MindScramblers Books

Becoming a Sales Magician

Becoming a Sales Magician

The Secrets Revealed

Christopher Lee Tabora

Published in the United States by MindScramblers Books
Printed by CreateSpace
Available from Amazon.com and other online stores.
Available soon on Kindle and other devices.
ISBN: 978-0-9960677-0-6 Print edition

I am grateful for Max Maven's permission to use his egg effect on page 60. Max retains copyright and all its privileges. The reader may use the effect for non-commercial applications only.

To my wife

the greatest magician

Acknowledgements

No author produces a book without the kind support from family, friends, and colleagues. My wife, Michele, and my children Emilee, Alexandra, and Trent, thank you for your sacrifice and patience. Mom, thank you for always believing in me, and my Lolo – Benigno Tabora – you are always an inspiration. Dad, thanks for teaching me the secrets to living life to the fullest.

I appreciate the work of my editor Nathan J. Barnes and my graphic designer Jordan Jones, and I especially thank David Chmielewski for the friendship, hard work, and photography he has selflessly contributed, and Danielle Langford who helped unveil the sculptor in me.

I am forever grateful for Leo Behnke, Bob Fitch, Tom Gaudette, and the countless other magicians that have helped me develop my craft. And to my many customers: without our indestructible relationships, this book would have never existed.

Thank you all.

Contents

Enriching Your Sales Experience

When I think about this process, I think of being back at school. Thankfully, the MAGIC method is the school of the never-ending snow day. Yes, in some school districts, kids get to enjoy a day or two out of school in which time they always study. They would actually be studying if by doing so they could exponentially increase their sales.

Who's driving the bus? If you don't, who will?

Foreword

I first met Chris in 1989 when he confidently strode in for his interview at the optical shop that was one of a chain in Connecticut I managed at the time. Fresh faced, barely out of school, and eager to take on a new chapter in life, his enthusiasm was contagious. While he had absolutely no training in the optical field, not to mention little sales experience, it was immediately clear we had ourselves a new hire that was born to sell.

He proved to be a quick study and within a month or two became the #1 sales person in the chain, instrumental in recreating the packages we offered, helping us to define and tailor them to the patients' needs. Chris and I worked together for several years; he was promoted through the ranks of both the company where we met and subsequently, a national chain where I moved and recruited him. While Chris has remained on the East coast, moving on to an extremely successful sales career in the medical device field, mine took me to the West coast, but we've always kept in touch.

Over the 25 years I've had the pleasure of knowing Chris, I've always been amazed by his uncanny ability to draw people in so deftly yet genuinely and convey his desire to connect with them on a deeper level, quickly gaining their trust. I've watched in awe again and again over the years as he drew crowds with simple coin and playing card sleight of hand, captivating the audience while engaging in light banter with them.

So the concept of using his finely honed magic skills to accentuate his remarkable ability to engage fellow human beings to create indestructible relationships is perfectly natural. The result is this fabulous how-to sales primer. You'll find plenty of personal stories, anecdotes, and tangible examples of situations where this talent proved critical to developing what Chris terms partnerships with his customers where he leads them to a clear understanding of their issue, and together they reach the conclusion that his product is the ultimate solution for the problem.

Having spent my career in sales, managing sales teams, or in brand and product marketing, while reading this I find myself drawn in and repeatedly relating to the basic tenets Chris lays out in this book. I've used many of them in my own process, but would have benefitted from having started out with this guidebook if only Chris had written it 30 years ago! In these pages, he outlines a succinct and simple step-by-step method based on what he calls the Three Pillars: *reading, preparation*, and *study* to help sales people develop what he terms 'indestructible' relationships. At the end of each chapter, there is a short exercise to drive home the key points in the previous pages to ensure understanding and effectively imprint them, slowly instilling in you new sales 'habits.'

To help you comprehend and retain the principles involved, Chris uses a bit of psychology, teaches some body language through gestures, and instructs on the fine art of listening. I am certain that you'll find them immensely helpful in assuring the development of your own solid partnerships that will become indestructible relationships. He places strong emphasis on listening, which I wholeheartedly endorse. Over the years I've always lived by the adage that you have two ears and only one mouth for a reason! Chris walks you through the truly successful salesperson's technique of active listening as a critical tool, quite clearly capturing and elucidating the difference between listening and really hearing.

I'm proud to see the career success of the young man that I met so many years ago. I'm also quite confident that the time spent reading this, learning the secrets Chris unlocks for you, and thoughtfully completing both the exercises in each chapter as well as the workbook at the conclusion will serve you very well in your quest to develop your own indestructible relationships, leading to fulfilling sales for you and a positive experience for your partners.

Nancy Roellke
Director of Category Management and Business Development
Acme Made Brand

My mind is the key that sets me free.

- Harry Houdini

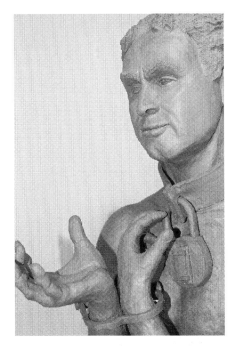

Harry Houdini, born Erik Weisz, was the master magician of the twentieth century. Even today, his name still rings as a recognizable icon in almost every household worldwide. His daring escapes forged him into the realm of American legend. Every magician seeks to build a similar personal brand. As a salesperson, you have your own personal brand to create... your own footprint.

How do you want your customers to remember you?

Chapter 1

Making Magic in Sales

Want to sell like Houdini?

By opening this book, you are taking the first step in proving what I feel to be a very valid point: *magic sells.* Don't worry, you are not alone. Unwavering interest in magicians and the art of magic has been vibrant for centuries. But think long and hard before you keep reading: people are typically disappointed when they find out how the tricks are done. It's usually much more enjoyable not knowing how these miracles are created. Sometimes the magic vanishes when the mysteries are revealed. The sales method described in this book is built on a tried and tested system. Coupled with a lifetime of magical studies, this method is a compilation of the many different sales systems that I have studied throughout my many years in the sales industry. Even with over two decades of selling numerous products and services at many different levels, I continue to learn more every single day about the secrets of using magic in sales.

The ideas presented in this book are not new, but are supercharged with the secrets of magic. Some salespeople might already be doing this stuff, but the secrets of magic will breathe new life into familiar practices. This method is alive because it speaks to the heart of effective sales—and one of the most important things in life—cultivating indestructible connections with other people. Indestructible connections are built on interacting, bonding, sharing, and understanding of other human beings. Knowing how to effectively cultivate these connections is paramount to developing the strong relationships that produce impressive sales results.

It's very easy to forget how important genuine personal relationships are to our health and success. The connections that people establish through all of the social media outlets are superficial and often detract from healthy relationships. If we take the time to connect and really understand people, these relationships can work for both magicians and salespeople in unimaginably powerful ways.

In this book, we are going to unlock the secrets of magic, the building blocks that helped me formulate the MAGIC method, a five-step process that helps salespeople connect with their customers, enabling them to develop lasting relationships that produce strong sales. Should you decide to continue reading and complete the exercises outlined in the workbook section, you will thoroughly understand this system and be ready to begin putting it into practice immediately.

Proper use of these tools will enable you to realize your interpersonal and financial goals at lightning speed. My vision is to assist you in acquiring these tools in the quickest, most efficient manner possible and in such a way that you are able to navigate through the system without having to think about it.

The goal is for you to integrate this method into your new positive "habit-forming" way of life. This is something that becomes part of you and who you are on a daily basis. Magicians refer to transformations like this as getting bit by the *magic bug*. Once this *magic bug* bites you... it's virtually impossible to get rid of it.

Now what do we mean by magic? When people think of a magician, they sometimes think of a guy in a tuxedo with tails, pulling a rabbit out of a hat. Of course, I have nothing against the magician who does these tricks—just as there are different kinds of salespeople, there are different categories of magicians. Most folks have grown up their entire lives hearing of magicians doing 'magic tricks,' and recall the guy who recently performed at their nephew's last party. I admire the magician who can capture the imagination of children at a birthday party, but the kind of magic we're talking about in this book embraces the sophisticated unpredictability of adult audiences. I have found that successful sales and an effective magic show have a lot in common, and knowing the secrets of magic have given me a tremendous advantage in sales.

A good salesperson, like a good magician, knows how to create the illusion of making the impossible a reality.

Birth of a Magician

It starts out the same way for almost every magician. It usually begins when a child receives his or her first magic set as a gift. This kid quickly fashions together an acceptable costume—a top hat, white gloves, and a wand—and relentlessly performs his or her version of classic magic tricks for all of the family and friends who are willing to watch. Some inadequacies in the performance are expected. No little kid can possibly be expected to fully decipher the atlas-sized encyclopedia of directions. Wonderful cheers and jeers of amazement abound from the generously polite adults. Clapping, ooohs and ahhhs... it's candy for the budding stage entertainer.

But there's always that one mean-spirited individual, typically an older sibling, who feels the need to point out their theory of how easily the miracle can be explained away. They do so publicly while unknowingly chipping away a little fragment of the aspiring young performer's self-esteem. Here the child has at least two courses of action: become a pyromaniac and burn the magic kit outside in the woods the next time his or her parents aren't around, or stay the course. I chose both, but the first part is a story best left untold.

Now a very small fraction of these little performers never burn... or retire their $19.95 cardboard and plastic "magic" kit to the back of the closet, like most "normal" kids. That decision marks the beginning of a lifelong journey, and a magician is born.

I'd like to think that I've come a long way from the plastic "magic kit," with my old top hat and cape. I actually put a lot of thought into my costume and the nature of my performances. Some of the finest choreographers in the business have worked with me, making sure that my team and I stay on the cutting edge. Because of this, our costumes were sometimes dated. I have to laugh at some of the things that we've done—the girls have had big, colored hair, the guys have gone shirtless with tight leather pants. We've looked more like a gothic Brady Bunch rather than a magic troupe with our flamboyant, matching attire.

Magic and Success

The highest grossing entertainer in history is the magician David Copperfield, the guy who made the Statue of Liberty disappear and walked through the Great Wall of China. Most people don't know the level of success that Copperfield enjoys. Just to put things in perspective: Michael Jackson was worth about $600 million. Tiger Woods is worth about $500 million dollars. Johnny Cash was worth about $120 million dollars. According to Forbes, David Copperfield has amassed a fortune of about $800 million dollars, and owns his own private cluster of islands in the Bahamas. In entertainment, he is second only to Opera Winfrey, who sits on a dazzling $2.8 billion. As a solo performer, Copperfield can rest easily knowing that his ticket sales are the highest in history at an unbelievable $4 billion. Plus, Opera could live a thousand lifetimes and never be able to cut herself in half like Copperfield (she's been trying for years).

Copperfield didn't become a superstar by being a lousy salesman. He created a very well thought out brand for himself that continues to sell astronomically today. Most importantly for us is this: he wasn't born a magician—nobody is. Copperfield fell in love with magic and dedicated his life to its secrets, and boy, did that pay off! But the story of magic doesn't begin or end with Copperfield's amazing success.

Cups and Balls

The theory behind the cups and balls is the cornerstone for the MAGIC method. The magician must master the art of capturing of interest and the imagination of the audience quickly—and hold it until the finale.

This effect is the pattern for successful sales: the salesperson must establish a connection and expertly guide the customer to the close—using the secrets of magic.

While it's not the oldest profession, magic is probably one of the oldest forms of entertainment. Some people think that a painting on the walls in the ruins in Beni Hasan, Egypt, documents what could be the oldest magic trick ever. The painting depicts a magician performing a cup and balls trick similar the effect that is a staple in the modern magician's show.

That same effect, the cups and balls, is still a staple in many of today's conjurer's repertoire. The same foundational trick just improved through the ages. This is true with most things in the world of magic. This can be applied to a lot of other different products and services as well. The concept of the trick is a constant while magicians through the ages have given it their own personal touch. Sales is just as old as magic, and sales methods are at least as old as the wheel. I imagine that the first caveman salesman, the discoverer of fire, used the principles of the first magician who was entertaining people with his cups and balls trick. Both appealed to emotion, used misdirection, and convinced their audience that their product could do something amazing. Both were successful when they stuck to their MAGIC method.

The *Work* of Magic

A good magician appears to make the impossible happen effortlessly. At least, that's the way it should look. In reality, the magician works tirelessly to master the craft. What is done in a moment in front of an audience can take years of practice before it is worthy to perform. All of the work is in the preparation.

You will notice that I am careful when to use the word *trick* and when to use the term *effect*. The word *trick* is associated with the stereotypical magician at a birthday party who pulls a little white bunny out of the hat. *A trick is the performance of magic without the need to bond with an audience and lead them through an effect.* The *trick* capitalizes on the cool factor, whereas an *effect* is designed to trigger an emotional impact. Magic tricks require little practice—they basically come in a kit. The process of reading, studying, and preparing is almost non-existent. If you follow the principles of performing a trick in your sales strategy, your sales pitch will be a gimmick. In sales, a polished professional's goal is to master his or her preparation. We aren't looking to scheme or deceive—quite the contrary—we want to build a lasting memory, a bond with our potential and current customers. We are going to build solid, indestructible relationships based on trust and the promise of mutual benefit.

An *effect*, however, takes years of practice. I explain this because I am trying to speak on behalf of magicians and explain that a majority of us are innovators, business owners, professional students, sales/marketing people, inventors, avid readers, professional speakers, actors, and dexterity specialists. We are fully dedicated to our craft. We devote years of our lives to all of these individual practices for a single moment... the moment that makes our targeted audience think... is that *really* magic?

This book isn't going teach you how to mesmerize a customer, getting them to close a deal without any effort on your part. The reason why my shows are successful is the careful thought and practice that my team and I invest in them. As a magician, I treasure the hard work that it takes to put together a show because I know that it will make the show memorable for the audience. As a salesperson, the more effective my preparation is, the more likely I'll connect with my customers and close the sale.

11

An important inspiration for my work ethic for both magic and sales comes from my *lolo*, which means "grandfather" in Filipino Tagalog. My lolo instilled the value of hard work, perseverance, sacrifice and most of all the opportunities that each one of us have before us in this great country—the United States of America. His name was Benigno Tabora, a Filipino who immigrated to the United States during World War II. He forsook a wealthy heritage in the Philippines to join the US Army as a Filipino scout to fight in the Pacific. He was captured by the Japanese and survived the Bataan Death March. He survived eight grueling months in a Japanese concentration camp where he was beaten, stabbed, and tortured regularly. He was moved from camp to camp, and even managed to escape twice. After the war, he made the courageous decision that would alter the course of his family forever. General MacArthur himself ensured safe transfer of the family. He settled in Fort Devens, Massachusetts and dedicated the next 31 years of his life to the United States Army, retiring in 1968 as a Sergeant Major, the highest rank possible for a foreign-born immigrant. He lived a full life because he worked hard every day of his 93 years, and that value is embraced in this book.

I went to visit my grandfather during the last week of his life, hoping to draw some wisdom from his final moments. As he lay there in bed, thin, frail and unable to move about as I was used to seeing him, instead of talking about his military days or his decorated career, some squirrels that were playing outside his window captivated him. Time and time again, as I tried to engage conversation towards historical aspects of the family, his attention wandered back to the squirrels. His movements were sparse and carefully calculated and his thoughts deep. He told me how important it was to him that I came to see him that day. And again his focus on the squirrels interrupted our conversation. He finally said to me, "You need to be like those squirrels." He only had the strength to tell me the basics of the most important lesson in life. The squirrels had to work all day, every day in order to survive. Winter had fully set in and the air was bitter, but even though they were scrambling to forage nuts to survive, they still managed to run and play and enjoy the task at hand. They were still dancing and playing while they were busy. That lesson has continued to resonate with me ever since. I honor my lolo by taking joy in the work of bringing smiles to peoples faces through the wonder of magic, and helping to enrich the lives of my customers by establishing indestructible relationships.

My lolo's lesson was basic, fundamental, and easy to remember. The magic of it is bound up in the profoundly complex experience of building strong human connections. Thank you, Lolo.

How to Use This Book

You don't need to know anything about magic—and not that much about sales—in order to fully apply the elements in this book. After all, this book is really about cultivating connections with other people, and if you can do that well, you can sell anything. One of the best things about this method is that it will teach you to think on your feet. You'll be able to more effectively anticipate the customer's needs, answer questions, and steer the pitch, all while keeping the customer's eye on the ball. This strategy will keep you from presenting a lifeless pitch that has become mundane because the joy of the sale has become monotonous.

I've seen this happen many times before, not just in sales, but also in magic. One particular magician, a very famous one, stands out quite vividly. I had the opportunity to see him perform in the early stages of his multi-year contract at a world-class casino, and I was blown away by the fantastic show he had put together. It was remarkable how well polished, engaging, and full of life he was.

Years later, towards the very end of his contract, I went to see him again. It was like seeing a totally different performer. His interaction with the audience was completely different. It was the same show with the same material, but it appeared as if he was "going through the motions" rather than performing miracles. The energy had left him.

Sometimes you need to step back and retool just to regroup and stay fresh and on top of your game, especially if you are using the same material over and over again.

The Tabora School of Magic

If you can identify your strengths first, you will have a springboard for a long, successful career in sales. The beauty of this method is that every aspect is carefully planned and connected, so the one or two elements that really come naturally to you will help strengthen everything else. Moving from strength is a very cool thing. Your strength is almost certainly different from your colleagues. The person who trained you might be exceptionally strong with knowing every last detail of every product that every competitor produces, or s/he might be exceptionally funny, or perhaps s/he knows how to capitalize on his/her attractive appearance. A salesperson needs to discover their strengths quickly and learn how to exploit these strengths to connect with the customer—that is what it means to move from strength. The easiest way to discover your strengths is to examine your interests.

Starting from one's interests can yield unexpectedly pleasant results. This book follows the Montessori approach to education, which encourages children to follow their interests. While our children were attending a Montessori school, my wife and I discovered that education is not something that the teacher does, but that it is a natural process that develops spontaneously in the human being. It is in the wonder of this natural process that the teacher can connect with the student and teach them the lessons that they need. A certain openness happens when children can be their true selves, following their genuine interests. As adults we can take full advantage of this principle.

Such an education can produce some unexpected results. I have an example to illustrate this point. One day my wife and I saw an unusual picture hanging on our three-year-old daughter's door.

We had no idea what it meant, so we had to ask her what was going on. She explained that she was upset with her little brother and wanted to keep him out of her room. After she told us what it was, the image became clearer. My three-year-old daughter had hung a sign outside her door declaring, "NO TRENTS!" Trent, her younger brother, was unwelcome in her room! Of course, we asked her how her little brother would feel if he understood the drawing. Thankfully, she took the sign down herself and eventually let her little brother play in her room again.

As a dad, I was surprised, impressed, and a little proud of her. She was able to draw his picture, cross it out, and write "No" so her one-year-old brother could read it and know that he better not come into her room. It was one of those times when you can't do much as a parent other than laugh. I wanted to hang it on the fridge, but the picture above is enough for me to remember. Why do I mention this story here? My three-year-old daughter developed her writing skills quickly because of her Montessori education. She has a love of learning, a strong sense of independence, and determination to achieve her goals, whatever they may be. We continue to see this translate to many other aspirations she gets in her mind. Her creative thinking is relentless, as at times so is her personality. She is very strong-willed because she is very self-confident, which is a reoccurring theme that I see in many of her Montessori peers.

As you may have guessed, I am an apostle of the Montessori method. You may know that in the early 19th century, the Italian educator Maria Montessori had a vision to educate children while respecting their interests and development. The central core of the Montessori way is to *follow the child* rather than *lead the child*. I love it because every part of the school is specifically designed for kids—everything is easily accessible to kids, not adults. So the sink that the kids use to wash dishes is smaller and lower—yes, they actually use real glass dishes and the floors are hard. The theory is by doing so, when the children drop one they learn the repercussion of doing so. They learn that it is fragile and can break, and they also learn how to sweep up and take care of the mess. The toilets are smaller, and all the furnishings are kid friendly. Walk into a public elementary school and you'll see smaller desks and chairs, but you won't see kids learning on their own terms. In a

Montessori classroom, older kids and younger kids learn together and teach each other. While students can pursue sensorial, mathematical, or practical life lessons, the enrichment of their interests leads to better performance in the rest of the program. Montessori students learn more content more effectively at a younger age. Success in one's interests and natural strengths is a powerful motivator. During this critical stage of development, it is comforting to know that my child's education is focused completely on them and not a test, more money from the government, or anything else that takes attention away from the kids. The belief is the knowledge children need should be absorbed naturally vs. relying and accumulating all of it directly from one source - the teacher. I take pride in the fact that my children and I are both products of Montessori schools.

The practical application of this method for you is that some of the elements in this book will be easier to understand and practice than others, but the entire program is designed so that you can use your more natural strength to expand your own personal sales skill set.

Why Do People Buy?

The funny thing about magicians is that we spend a majority of our time thinking about what would be cool for others to see and experience. We try to out figure out how to best present that as a miracle, or how to best inspire wonder, or freak people out the most, and then come up with a way to make that happen.

The magician is the most honest of all professions. He first promises to deceive you, and then he does.
Magician Karl Germain

Audiences want to see the magician make the impossible happen. They know that the magician is going to deceive them, and when the magician is successful, they love it. Maybe there's a streak of self-aggrandizement that the magician destroys: people think that it's more difficult to deceive them than it actually is, so they are impressed when a magician appears to deceive them effortlessly. Another interesting thing magicians have discovered is that the more intelligent the audience is, the easier it is to fool them. I'd much rather perform for a group of doctors, engineers, or lawyers than any other types of individuals. The furrowed brows and open mouths from such highly educated individuals are priceless.

Customers need the impossible to happen as well. The ethical salesperson—or the salesperson who wants to have a long-lasting career—does not deceive his/her customers. This is not true for magic. However, the customer must be convinced that the salesperson's product best meets their needs in spite of their own skepticism and mistrust. Our customers will certainly think that they are more difficult to convince than the average person, and the salesperson who is savvy enough to navigate through their critical mind—especially without the customer realizing it—is doing the impossible.

Now please understand that the illusion is sometimes not an actual illusion, but your mind building an illusion within itself. Sometimes that illusion that you create in your mind becomes a major inhibitor or distractor from you realizing your goals. Take for instance fire-walking. Yes... walking on red-hot burning coals.

Walking on hot coals is something that you can learn. This isn't a process that comes to mind on a daily basis with most conservative, level-headed individuals, but it is definitely cool. You shouldn't try this on your own; people need to be taught how to do this. Everything is real: the fire, your feet, your fear. When my wife and I were learning how to fire-walk, she suffered a minor burn that healed very quickly. The event was a success, and we enjoyed it so much that we went through formal training. We have been trained on how to orchestrate a fire-walk.

If you haven't attended a fire-walking workshop, it will do you a lot of good. How many of your competitors know how to walk on hot coals? The advantage is clear—once you've done that, you'll be able to handle the most challenging customers and the most intense circumstances. If you're in any ordinary sales position, these two challenges often intersect—you really, really want the sale and the customer will be playing hard to get, even if both you and the customer know that you are selling the best product to meet their needs. So what does a magician do to prepare for a hostile audience when everything is on the line? The magician becomes a student of the human mind, and because of that, the magician can walk on fire.

Reading, Study, and Preparation

Connecting with other people takes some work, and we salespeople have to do even more work to connect with the wide variety of people that we meet in a sales call. Fortunately, the MAGIC method is not complex, but it also isn't simple or easy. Its effectiveness depends on honest, hard work, but the method makes your work more fruitful.

The MAGIC method is built on three pillars that are the groundwork for connecting with customers. In fact, these three pillars are important for success in almost any profession. The development of any profession requires *reading*, *study*, and *preparation*. These three pillars will help you to get the most out of the MAGIC method, and get you on your way to exponentially increasing your sales.

Reading

The first pillar of the MAGIC method is *reading*. When I developed an interest in magic—and in sales—I quickly discovered that reading a good amount of quality material was absolutely essential to my success. Magic and sales overlap significantly because the way that a magician connects with audiences and the way that a salesperson connects with customers are fundamentally the same. Over the years, I've built a library with more than ten thousand volumes on topics related to magic and sales—that's as much as my house can hold, and as much as my wife will tolerate. A magician has to buy a lot of books because they are rare and magic is such a secretive art. Some books are only printed in extremely small batches, can cost thousands of dollars, and magicians tend to keep them under lock and key. Spouses of magicians have a special place in magic heaven, but most of them cannot resist rolling their eyes as their partner talks about the next magic book they *really must have.*

Salespeople naturally drift towards obvious books on motivation and business. There are some fantastic books on these topics, but that's only one part of the game. If sales is like war, some light reading is like going to battle in a T-shirt and a broomstick. When we go to battle, we want every advantage— all of the power of the Air Force and Navy, the best aerial surveillance, and most of all, the Marine and his rifle. We want to learn everything we can about the human psyche, gestures, personalities, neuroscience, and everything else that you can use to help you discover the secrets of human connection.

If you read two books a week, every week of every month of every year, you will slowly become an expert and develop the ability to read people and navigate a room with the precision of a stealth bomber pilot.

Study

About 3/4ths of what I read doesn't stick. So most of what I read the first time just leaves me. Gone. I might even say that I lose 7/8ths. The thing is, I don't remember how much I can't remember. Fortunately, the brain is a wonderful thing, and even if we don't remember what we've read, it's not really lost. It's a matter of access. *Study* is the method that I use to access the 3/4ths of the material that I lost when I read it the first time. There are very few of us with photographic memory who can read something once and retain 100% of what we've read; it's impressive to me to get above the 35% mark. Let's be honest, if someone could do this, they probably wouldn't be reading this book, they would definitely not be in sales, and their name would probably be *Wikipedia*.

The second pillar for the MAGIC method is *study*. The difference between reading and study is that reading is the exercise of familiarizing yourself with the content of a book. Study is when you spend time with the book, taking notes, coming back to it several times so you can commit its contents to memory.

It's that serious. In order to really know the material well enough to use it, we can't merely scan through a stack of books. We need to be able to identify valuable information and really think through it carefully. How do we know what is valuable? It's valuable when we find ourselves using the information while we work. Then, we can come back to the source, read it again, and learn more. It needs to become a part of our souls.

Now the reward is cool. Studying will enable us to respond to an unexpected situation without thinking. In a way, all we're doing is preparing for a sale—in the sense that it's all that we do all the time. In another sense, we'll never have to prepare for a sale ever again because we will be using the secrets of magic to make good sales strategies part of who we are. We won't need to think about what we're doing in a presentation because we have thought about everything beforehand. That's what study does for us. That's what it means to be prepared for a presentation. The magician relentlessly practices and polishes every flourish, footstep, and facial expression, timing every movement of his/her body to the second in order to perform flawlessly. When the moment finally arrives and the effect captures the imagination of the audience, magic is alive.

Genuine magic depends on perfect simplicity of execution.
Magician Jean Hugard

Preparation

The performance of magic *under fire* is unforgiving. The term *under fire* in magic refers to the performance of an effect before an audience who can roast him/her if they fail. It's happened before, and it kills careers. The integrity of the magician leans hard on the idea that s/he is a flawless superhuman who makes the impossible happen. There are comic magicians whose act is driven by self-deprecation; in this case, they focus on making themselves the joke instead of joking with the audience. The self-depreciating magician practices his or her timing, rhythm, and staging to the extent that his/her well-thought-out and precisely executed movements seem impromptu. Most magicians are perfectionists who must plan, practice, and execute every part of their act down to the minute detail. This does not mean that the magician is always perfect, but he/she *appears* in control even when things are unexpected. A seasoned magician can anticipate the unexpected and make it seem like a part of the show.

The third pillar for the MAGIC method is *preparation.* Like a "magic show," a sales pitch is performance under fire. Some good news for you—one encouraging point among many—is that sales is a bit more forgiving than magic. During the sales pitch, there is more opportunity to correct oneself, more opportunity for recovery. As a salesperson, you need to make the impossible happen, but you do it within the context of a genuine human connection. This connection can be difficult to establish. You may be a natural salesperson who can immediately and effortlessly connect with your customers. Most of us need to rely on misdirection, making the most out of what we can gather from our customers' reactions to us through what they say and their body language.

Every time the magician takes the stage, their reputation is on the line. If a show goes sideways, it can mean the end of a career. Imagine if David Copperfield spent all of that money on hype, telling the world that he would make the Statue of Liberty disappear, only to fail to deliver? There's no recovery from that. Because of this very real risk, the magician is highly motivated to prepare for the show.

Many people believe that sales is a gift that a minority of people have, and the rest of us are hopeless. These gifted people aren't motivated to prepare or practice their craft outside of the sales call. Usually, it's true that the most successful salespeople have the personality and charisma that simply cannot be taught, and it can barely be explained. I know a salesperson that has consistently been number 1 or 2 in his company for more than 20 consecutive years. This guy is a rock star in the sales industry. And he lives like a rock star. This guy parties like I have never seen anyone party before.... nightly.... for the past 25 years straight. We all know the type. He strolls in tanked, smelling like cigars, eyes half-shut, and slurring his words at 3am every night of the sales meetings and is the first guy sitting in the meetings just four hours later, bright-eyed and ready to rock. Even though there must be a toothpick holding his eyelids open, he's sitting on the front row with a big smile on his face. How he does it, I have no idea, but I have all the respect in the world for how he manages to produce at the level that he does.

I have another friend who is the COO of a company—he grew up in sales—and he still makes a ton of sales. He's a very good-looking guy who used to be a professional football player, and he's still in very good shape. He's also very smart, which is an odd match for such an overbearing man. But he's a natural master at reading a room. He can size up a personality instantly and make a customer feel instantly comfortable and *want to* have a good, friendly conversation. The customer closed the deal before they even shook the guy's hand.

No one taught my friend how to sell. If he had made an effort to change anything that he already did, it might have hindered his success. He simply learned about the product a little, and people are almost completely defenseless against the power of his sales kung-fu. Some salespeople are blessed with the good looks and charisma that truly give them an advantage. It's a fundamental truth in life that kittens have it easy. There's something about a cute little ball of fluff that melts the heart. And seriously, would we really put up with cats if they weren't kittens first? At least we can remember when they were cute when they pee on the rug, not as an accident, but out of spite because we didn't come home from work on time? Many puppies wouldn't make it through their first year if they didn't look up at you with those devastatingly helpless eyes.

A magician is an actor playing the part of a magician.
Jean Eugène Robert-Houdin

This is where magic and sales differ. No good magician is a natural. Jean Eugène Robert-Houdin (1805-1871) is considered the father of modern magic, and thousands of magicians after him have embraced this axiom as the guiding inspiration of their work. A *magician* is simply an actor playing the role of a magician. I'm hoping that by the end of this book you have enough knowledge to start producing some magic of your own. My goal is to make you an outstanding magician actor. The person learning magic is also a magician. You don't suddenly become a magician when you've mastered the art. You begin there and work your way up. So even now you can consider yourself a sales magician.

The art of illusion is only achieved through reading, study, and practice. A magician does not innately know how to read an audience, anticipate what they will believe, and craft an effect designed to flawlessly entertain an audience. This only occurs through experience. And this is what you will gain from this book: the way to practice good sales preparation and technique when it is not already in your blood. How do you know if you're not a natural? You're a born natural if you're the person on your sales team who can sell without selling. If you can do that, you've already arrived. Most of us are not there yet, but this level of success is within your reach if you read, study, and practice.

So you can have it by nature, or you can develop it through nurture. Most of us need a lot more than our furry pelt and a wagging tail to make things happen. You might not be a Golden retriever puppy, but the secrets of magic can make you look like one to your customer, even if you're a full-grown mastiff.

Nurture begins with reading, is enhanced by study, and perfected through preparation. Preparation that is based on reading and study is the complete opposite of preparing a scripted sales pitch. Reading and study entails learning about human nature that will help you think on your feet and make the impossible a reality for your customers.

A magician has to plan everything down to the smallest movement, having a plan for recovery for almost every possible scenario. A new effect can take years for a magician to perfect. Some card effects can take more than *five years* to master, and perhaps even longer to perfect the techniques one needs to both misdirect the audience and complete the full effect. And even after years of practice, the magician needs to be prepared for things to go wrong under fire. I used to perform an effect that capitalizes on this truth.

First, I fanned out a deck of cards, and asked a volunteer to pick one, memorize it without allowing anyone else see it, and put it back into the deck. Then I casually mix the cards—or even better, ask them to do it. After the cards are sufficiently mixed, I asked them to cut it and take a peek at the top card to see if their card is showing. More than 99% of the time, it would be the wrong card. Now, the magician knows that people really want to root for the underdog in these situations. They want you to succeed. I'd repeat the entire process again with the same result. This usually results in some groans and at times a sympathetic, "it's alright" from the crowd. I then ask the audience if they know what our fine State of Connecticut is famous for. They're typically dumbfounded by the question. So, I'd reply - it's the insurance capital of the world. Then, I pull out an insurance policy out of my coat pocket with their original card printed jumbo-sized on the inside of it. This effect has great appeal. The audience felt bad for me when I appeared to fail, and then they are blown away. The audience was taken by surprise when I redeemed myself. However, an absolute miracle occurred in those rare instances when luck was on my side and their card ends up on the top of the deck the first time. It's difficult to anticipate every little thing that can go wrong in a sale, but if we know the secrets of the MAGIC method, we can recover easily from the unexpected.

Misdirection

The performance of magic depends on mastering the art of misdirection. It is usually impossible to successfully perform an effect without some form of misdirection whether it is visual, physical, or psychological. Unfortunately, misdirection will fail when someone attempts it without careful practice.

I once saw a novice magician adding flourishes and card fans to show off his card dexterity to the audience. Unable to bridle his ego, he felt the need to show off. When he performed a card trick for the audience, his sleight of hand misdirection was ineffective, and he was caught by a couple of the audience members. By showing off his card handling, he made them feel like they needed to watch his every move. This was a big mistake on his part.

Some were guessing incorrectly about his technique and were convinced they were correct. It didn't matter whether they were wrong or right... the damage had been done. A potential miracle was reduced to being a simple puzzle. I've seen this happen time and time again to young magicians. Contrary to their belief, if the audience has no idea of how well you can manipulate cards, they won't watch you as closely, and they are easier to misdirect.

It is very important to know that *misdirection* is not *maleficent deception*. It's not a lie that is intended to harm, but a directing that is in the other person's favor. As we saw in the insurance effect discussed above, at a performance of magic the audience expects the magician to deceive them—for their own entertainment. So they receive the benefit that they expected. The customer wants to know all of the great things about your product–how it can enrich their lives and make things easier for them–so keeping their attention on the topic that they want to hear about gives them what they want. I'll carefully note that misdirection in selling is not feature selling. We should avoid telling the customer every feature, every bell and whistle, that our shiny new trinket has to offer. It may work when selling a value meal, but it's a sure-fire way to fail in a larger sale. I'm talking about using the art of misdirection to guide the conversation to what the customer needs and wants to hear: only the features of the product that make their lives easier and enrich their lives—and keeping the conversation from going anywhere else.

Misdirection is simply the art of steering the audience's attention to where the magician needs in order to create the effect. For the salesperson, misdirection is the art of steering the sales pitch so that his or her buyers focus on the value of the product and the good that it will do for them. The biggest mistake in sales, particularly for newbies, is the *blah, blah, blah* syndrome. They just talk and talk and talk, spilling all of the information about their product, thoughtlessly spitting out mundane details that the customer could care less about.

On a personal note, I've found that the magician and the salesperson sometimes deal with some internal guilt because they depend so heavily on the practice of misdirection. Following and believing your imagination is key here. If the magician has a sensitive conscience, the entire show becomes an unbearable lie. And this is a lie that the audience can easily detect. The magician has to fool him/her self. For instance, if a magician pretends to place a coin into his/her other hand, but palms the coin, s/he has to firmly believe that the coin is in the hand s/he is pretending it to be in. If there is any doubt, even a subtle flinch, the spectator can sense this. The magician has to learn to believe that he or she is performing real magic. If the magician thinks that s/he is "lying" about the location of the coin, then every misdirection is a lie. This unfortunate soul will descend in a downward spiral. Every show will get worse until s/he gives up completely.

Salespeople can experience a sensitive conscience under usual circumstances, but if you find yourself moving from using misdirection to steer a sales call to defining the sales call, you are in a very dark place. This usually means that you cannot find any advantage about your product or service that you can direct your customer to, and you've given in to the idea the competition is better in all respects. However, constructive misdirection is a characteristic of good sales. Positive uses of misdirection are:

• Keeping the customer focused on the good qualities of the product

• Asking leading questions to get the customer to open up, even if you know the answers

• Eliminating physical barriers

• Asking leading questions about what they are currently using so they feed you information about disadvantages of competition that you may already know

For both the magician and the salesperson, the solution to a sensitive conscience is that you truly need to believe that you're the "good guy." The magician needs to know that the coin is really in the other hand. A magician prepares for a show like an actor prepares for a part. We all know the terms that actors have for this: "in character" and "out of character." Heath Ledger got so into his Joker character for his Batman movie that he said that he had nightmares about it. If an actor is out of character in a movie, it's not any fun to watch – unless it's Michael Douglas or a Mike Tyson cameo. We didn't pay to see them being themselves. Think about it: have you ever seen an actor speak as him or herself? Most of the time it pales in comparison to the wonderful performance that they give in the movies, where their words are scripted, they are directed, and the final product is edited. When actors forget who they are supposed to be, the illusion fails. When a magician is in character, the magician has to truly believe that he or she is doing magic. If the magician ceases to believe, he or she falls out of character and the show no longer features a magician.

The salesperson needs to truly believe and *know* that he or she is the "good guy" or "good girl." Self-belief is the only way that the performer can be persuasive. We may be tempted to think that there are more negatives than positives to our product or service, the competition might seem better, and we might be certain that we don't have a chance against a competing sales person. The secret to avoid falling into that trap is knowing that there is always one thing that your product can do that no one else can do. An old Kung Fu instructor taught his students that if you develop one punch or kick—work on power, timing, and speed, you can hit anyone with that technique. If we learn to believe in our products and ourselves, we at least have the best possible chance—and we will win more sales.

Card mechanics and dice hustlers are experts at misdirection. The foundational components of many magicians' conjuring techniques stems from the work of these very daring individuals. I had the opportunity to meet one of the last greats through a close mutual friend. His name is "Fast Jack." There is a fantastic biography on his adventures. Mr. Farrell worked for many years as a dice hustler and gaming cheat for a diverse crowd spanning from Wall Street moguls to mafia dons. Although he now says he wouldn't travel the same path again, he was able to enjoy unparalleled success for decades. His dexterity, talent, and strong belief that what he was doing was justified were the key elements to his success. Webster's Dictionary should include a picture of him beside the word self-confidence.

One of the purposes of misdirection is to be in control even though it appears that you're not—and appear not to be in control when you really are. Even when things don't go as planned, the secrets of magic enable you to integrate the unexpected into your presentation. A show is never without flaws that the audience thinks is part of the act.

There are conventional rules of sales that are designed to keep the salesperson in control of the call. We're told not to let our customers handle the product until we are 3/4ths though the pitch. Once the product is in the customer's hands, the salesperson may as well not even be in the room. The customer loses all interest in the pitch and focuses all of their attention on the product. This isn't a good thing because the customer won't hear all the great things that we have to say about the product. They may even find something they don't like about your product before you have the opportunity to share the one magical thing that resolves all of their issues. During the pitch, you should ask leading questions about what they like about or would change about their current products—you are going to let them give you information that you already know. But they are going to tell you what is the most important thing to them. They will reveal the hot button to success. Let them help clear the path to your success.

Sometimes there are elements of the sales call in that path that requires you to take control. When you walk into a room, there may be physical barriers—like a desk, for example—that come between you and the customers. To gain control over this challenge, you can position your laptop or tablet away from the customer and invite them over to sit by you to get a better view. Less physical barriers mean a more direct path.

Personality Types

To cultivate indestructible connections, the salesperson must be a master at identifying personality types and giving them what they need. Not only will this help you with sales, but it can be a foundational aspect of building stronger personal relationships in every aspect of your life. You don't need to be a Rhodes

Scholar or a psychiatrist to determine a personality type with enough accuracy to make a powerful impact on your sales. For the purposes of this book, we are looking for four general personality types (based on Merrill and Reid, *Personal Styles and Effective Performance*). I like to remember their categories in the following format:

The egg-based personality menu

Poached Egg *engineered for efficiency*	**Hard-Boiled Egg** *tough and solid*
Over Easy Egg *warm disposition*	**Sunny-Side Up Egg** *life of the party*

I know that I'm speaking Sanskrit now, but this is really easy. According to Merrill and Reid (which almost every sales writer follows), there are four personality types. And I happen to love eggs—whether they are hard boiled, over easy, sunny side up, or even poached. I'm friends with all kinds of eggs, but these are the four general types. It's easy to remember four, right? When you walk into a room, you'll remember what to look for if you know the four types of eggs. The **Hard Boiled Egg** is tough on the outside and solid through the middle. The **Hard Boiled Eggs** are the directors, the Type A drivers who want the facts presented directly. They aren't always in tune with their emotions and other's thoughts on things. **Hard Boiled Eggs** are mostly concerned with getting results as fast as possible. **Hard Boiled Eggs** are typically in leadership positions, but beware: they aren't always presidents, CEOs, or even department heads. They can be disguised as assistants, folks from the business office, or anyone else in the room. In fact, personality type does not dictate a person's level of success—any personality can take on any role. Whatever their position in the company, **Hard Boiled Eggs** have a very low tolerance for BS and small talk.

Sunny-side Up Eggs like to party. They are very social and expressive, talk with their hands, and are very emotive. They don't like to be held down by the technicalities of everything. **Sunny-side Up Eggs** make sure everyone is having fun and enjoying themselves. They get the job done with the efficiency of a **Hard Boiled Egg**, but they want to have fun doing it. It's not a steadfast rule, but many salespeople tend to fall within this quadrant.

Then there's the **Poached Eggs,** folks who could care less about price; they are more interested in how things work. Many engineers fall into this category. They will ask you the most difficult questions about the product. This is what you study for, why you know your product inside and out. You don't learn everything about your product to saturate your customers with *blah*. You do all that work so you can answer difficult questions without thinking, telling your customers what they want to know. **Poached Eggs** are technical academics that want systems in place that bore the **Hard Boiled Eggs** (want to get the job done) and **Sunny-side Up Eggs** (want to have fun). While the **Poached Egg** may seem boring to the other two, the **Poached Egg** is probably thinking the **Sunny-side Up Egg** is as useful as a white crayon.

The **Over Easy Eggs** are—you guessed it—the folks who think with their feelings. They just want to get along with everyone. It's not price or functionality that will win their hearts. They want the salesperson to connect with them on an emotional level. They want to make sure that the entire group is happy, no stepping on toes, going outside of boundaries. **Over Easy Eggs** also like consistency and very low risk. They are more concerned about job security for everyone than doing something new. Due to their nurturing tendency, a lot of nurses tend to reside in this quadrant. Being diagonally across from the **Hard Boiled Eggs** makes them least adaptable to the unsympathizing nature of the **Hard Boiled Egg's** personality.

So there are four personalities, and anyone in the room *can* fit into one of these broad categories. Just like there are different kinds of eggs, there are four personality types that you should watch for in the office: the **Hard Boiled, Sunny-side Up, Over Easy,** and **Poached.** Piece of cake, right?

Identifying them is only half the battle. The other half is giving each personality what they need.

When you're able to identify personality types, you'll notice that they have a difficult time getting along with each other. The driven, fact-based **Hard Boiled Egg** might think that the emotive **Sunny-side Up Egg** is too engrossed in having a good time than pushing the work through at warp speed. The academic/engineer **Poached Egg** type doesn't care as much about money as some of the other types; they are primarily interested in how the product works and its efficiency. The salesperson needs to try to become a **Scrambled Egg,** being all things to all people, responding to the various dynamics that each personality brings into the room. If the **Sunny-side Up Egg** doesn't feel free to be expressive or sense that you are not confident in your product, you will have a difficult time making a sale. The **Over Easy Eggs** want to get along with everyone else, so what they get from you is important. The **Hard Boiled Egg** is the driver, but this person might not have the final say in a purchase. This is important to know - some **Over Easy Eggs** may allow the **Hard Boiled Egg** to control the meeting. The **Poached**

Egg isn't concerned with price as much as performance—these are the folks who will be paying careful attention to how much your product can do—the bang for the buck.

I do want to remind the reader that the four **Eggs** are general personality types. These general types are quite fluid; there's just as much variety in personality styles as there are people. Some folks may be completely one type all the time, some people may be mixed, and some folks may not fit at all.

The egg-based personality scramble

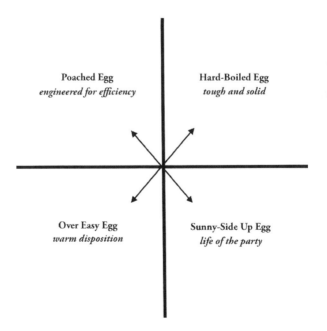

Poached Egg
engineered for efficiency

Hard-Boiled Egg
tough and solid

Over Easy Egg
warm disposition

Sunny-Side Up Egg
life of the party

Some folks are chameleons, able to take on the appearance of any given personality at any time. Within this great diversity, the goal for the salesperson is to develop a high level of versatility and respond to the customer appropriately no matter what type of egg they are. In a room full of different types of eggs, it is important to be able to navigate though the chart to meet each individual's demand.

You should always be on the lookout for the **Rotten Egg**, the one person that can spoil the entire group. This type of egg can show up spontaneously from any of the four quadrants. It might be that a **Hard Boiled**, **Sunny-side Up**, **Over Easy** and **Poached Egg** could just be having a bad day. Unfortunately, you will find that some people enjoy sabotage and chaos, thriving on being bad eggs.

There's a way to determine what kind of egg you are. On the next page you'll find a personality test of sorts. I have found it to be very accurate in discovering the personality types of friends, colleagues, and partners. Take just a moment to work through the questions and uncover your personality type. Ask yourself... what kind of an egg would I be?

Spin your wand.

How do you like *your* eggs?[†]

1. Take a peek at the dozen eggs on the next page. Each one is labeled as a different type of egg to indicate different types of personalities that we have. Among the different personalities there are brown (the darker) eggs and white (the lighter) eggs.

2. Select one of the ***white egg*** personality types and place your finger on it.

3. From there, I would like you to *slide your finger left or right, in the same row,* to the closest ***brown egg***. Once you are there keep you finger there.

4. Now, *move up or down in that column,* to the nearest ***white egg*** and keep your finger that egg.

5. Okay, this one is a little tricky. On this next move, I would like you to *move diagonally, one square only* to the nearest ***brown egg***. Perfect… again, keep your finger there–we are almost done.

6. Finally, the last set of instructions… *Move across, left or right in the same row,* to the nearest ***white egg*** and remember this egg.

[†] I am grateful to Max Maven for giving me permission to use his effect here. Max retains all copyright privileges and protections. The reader may use this effect for non-commercial purposes only.

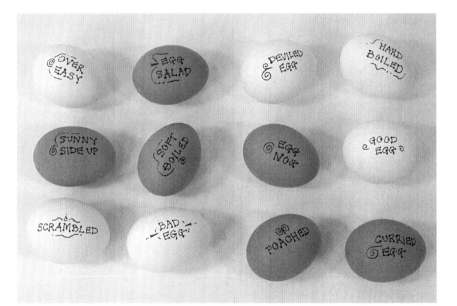

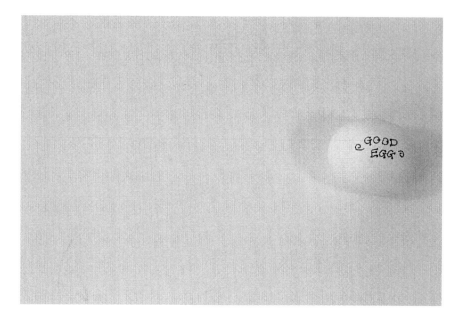

You should be on the type of egg personality we are striving to be. The Good Egg!

Chapter 1 Recap

- Magic's power in sales—#1 performer is David Copperfield
- Misdirection—leading call to focus on the good of your product
- Three pillars of MAGIC method—reading, study, and preparation
- Four personalities—**Hard Boiled**, **Sunny-side Up**, **Over Easy** and **Poached**

Magic for Thought

1. There are many different kinds of magicians—what kind are you?

2. What is a good use of misdirection in a sales pitch?

3. Have you ever really studied anything before? What was the payoff?

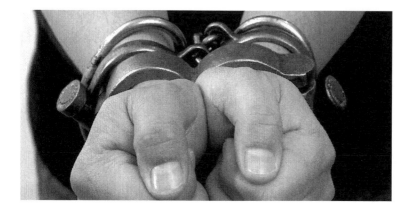

It's time to break free.

Chapter 2

Becoming a Sales Magician

Want to capture the imagination like Houdini?

Being a sales magician is something that will take some work, but the efforts are rewarding. As we said before, no magician is born—they are always raised. When you learn the secrets of magic, you'll look like a natural.

Because my interest in magic began at the age of seven, my professional sales traits evolved much later in life. However, the two of them have emerged as equally influential drivers for who I am today. My sales and management experience helped shape my magic career tremendously while also providing me with a very stable living for both me and my family. Could I have been a successful sales person without the magic background? Absolutely. Would I have been able to reach the pinnacles I have thus far and would it have been as easy and painless as it has been for me? I can say with conviction—definitely not. The two together shaped me.

Magic extends from children's parties to the corporate sector to television and the casinos. All require different approaches. The fundamentals are the same, but the landscapes are different. The higher levels require more sophisticated attention. The same goes for the sales process. Although all levels require a specialized art, the roots remain similar.

Fortunately, magic came first for me and helped open my eyes to all of the different characteristics within the sales process. Being involved with magic forced me to study the intricacies of how people think, how they react, and how they resist. Basically, it forced a general study of human psychology upon me. It took me quite some time to fully understand that there is one single elementary ingredient that highly propels success for both sales professionals and magicians alike. It isn't something that is blatantly obvious to the typical observer, but it is repeatedly mentioned in both schools of thought in their respective studies. To a small degree, I was aware of it from my own training on both sides, but it wasn't until I heard it first hand from a magician friend of mine, that I came to fully understand its importance to both industries. As a student of sales, I'm sure you have heard it many times as well. I hope it resonates with you much quicker than I was able to grasp it. The funny thing is that it is not a very complicated idea. It's actually quick and simple. This is what I learned:

My problem was that I "heard" it... but I failed to really "listen."

This chapter focuses on some preliminary practices that must be in place in order to practice the MAGIC method. In chapter one, I talked about the three pillars of the method: reading, study, and preparation. In this chapter, I will focus on listening and interacting with your customer.

Listening is Asking Leading Questions

The first secret of sales is learning how to craft questions that prompt an informative response rather than a simple yes or no answer. One example of a great way to do this is to ask someone *where they are and how did they get there.* This question embodies the principle of the leading question: asking questions that tell you more about the customer and their experiences than they would normally would reveal. The leading question allows us to steer the conversation in such a way that it builds a path of information that will hopefully lead to a sale. Please understand, this is much more than it appears on the surface—this is a personal exercise that gets easier and more valuable the more we practice. Crafting our own leading questions is something we can practice in our everyday conversations. We can try asking questions that prompt more than one word answers. When we master how to ask important questions disguised as small talk, our customers will connect with us without even realizing it. So we're not just asking a question; we are inviting ourselves to listen to our customers' stories, earning their trust, and discovering their understanding of their needs.

The purpose of the leading question is for us to connect with the customer on a personal level and convince them that our product will meet their needs. This particular question is an oversimplification of the casually innocuous icebreaker, "So, what do you do for a living?" In the United States, this is usually the first question that people ask each other when they are just getting to know someone. It's the way we decide how we are going to interact with strangers. Now, if you knew me, you would know that I carry my passion on my sleeve. That might sound melodramatic, but I never stop being a professional magician, and I never stop being a salesman. It's who I am, part of my being. And I'm one of those unfortunate souls who are expected to actually perform their job for free wherever I go. So I cringe when the person sitting next to me on a three-hour (or more!) flight asks me what I do for a living. I cringe because I know that my new friend is going to be asking me the same questions that people always ask me when they find out that they have the good fortune of sitting next to a goofball magician.

- Can you make my wife (husband, kid, whoever) disappear?
- What card am I thinking of?
- What am I thinking of right now?
- Do you do birthday parties? (followed by … 'My three-year-old's birthday is in a few weeks')
- Can you read my palm?

• Are *you* Chris Angel? (usually from drunk business executives)

It's impossible to have a conversation with someone who won't be happy unless you've proven that you can read their mind— or worse, they beg me to do something else miraculous.

There's no way to shut this off once it starts. I've actually slipped on my *Dr. Who* eye mask and gone to sleep only to wake up to see that Mr. Chatty McLoudmouth has been happily prattling on, I guess under the assumption that I could hear him through my *Dr. Dre Beats*, blasting vintage Van Halen - *Running with the Devil.* Perfect trip. An accountant would have been able to make talk about sports or movies or kids or something and then drift off into a book, a movie, or create a better mousetrap. Sigh.

If I ask them anything about themselves, I always get the same response, "I'll answer that question, but you'll have to show me something first." Now I love magic and I love to talk about it, but what people really want to know is what this book is about: the secrets of magic.

I had a priest sit next to me on a flight. I asked him about his job and I wanted to tell him my entire life's story. Instead,

I opted instead to ask him why he wasn't wearing a clerical collar—I figured he was a clergyman of a church that didn't use such vestments. He told me that he hated it when people talked with him the entire flight, confessing odd stuff, attempting to get his approval for this or that, and feigning interest in theology or philosophy. The old padre just wanted to take a nap. A kindred spirit! I finally felt comfortable revealing my secret identity. I told him I was a magician and he never left me alone.

There's just something about magic that instantly captures the imagination. It has an enduring popularity. It appeals to all ages and genders and crosses over into all cultures. Whether the person has an accurate or stereotypical view of what I do as a magician, it's more interesting than other things that people just can't talk about with such appeal—like crunching numbers for a corporation, working HR for a hospital, or shaving dogs at PetSmart. These are noble professions, but not good conversation material. People might pretend to be religious around a priest, but everyone knows that magicians can do some pretty cool stuff.

Eagerness to talk works in our favor. Asking people what they do and how they got there can lead them to open up and connect with us on a personal level. People like to tell their stories—they don't like to be interrupted by someone who wants to focus on the peripheral, surface level assumptions about their job. They want an active listener—someone who asks questions that indicate genuine interest. An active listener reinforces the speaker's belief that their climb to fame is genuinely interesting to them—and to us. It is important because it's their story, and knowing it will help us connect with them and cultivate an indestructible relationship. When we steer the conversation to their current products and their experiences with it—even if they are feeding us information that we already know—we are positioned to do the magic of connecting with our customers.

Making a Lasting Impression

In sales, it's important to be yourself. This is abundantly obvious, but still worth mentioning. We are not salespersons; we are people acting like salespersons. Salespersons are supposed to be 'in character,' but an important part of the character is you. You draw from your experiences to make the relational connections needed to become someone who focuses on his or her customer's needs and not just talking about the product.

We want to be remembered, not lost in the masses of "professional individuals" who stop in and rattle off the newest technological features and benefits of this year's widget. There are a whole slew of those people that knocked on your customer's door last week and the months prior. You want your customer to remember *you*, not just your products or services. You want to create the same level of impact that Houdini fashioned with his fans.

You have to build your own band of supporters by being yourself. After all, people do like you... that's why you are in sales in the first place... why try being someone you're not? Are you an automated robot? Of course not. You have an identity and a personality that differs from everyone else. Maybe you're a comedian, maybe you have some crazy outlandish hobby or talent... maybe you're a magician. Whatever it is... I'm positive of what you're not—you're definitely not just a monkey in a suit. But if you happen to have a monkey, bringing him along may be a creative marketing tactic.

Let's be clear, the message here isn't that we should walk into our next sales call and greet our potential customer by rattling off George Carlin's "Seven Filthy Words... Sh#%, Pi##, Fu#$, Cu*&, Co#$Suc$#@, Mother$%#$%er and Ti#$." I think most of us agree that we have to have some sort of a governor that tempers our thoughts to the situation. Mr. Carlin understood this. Imagine how short his stint as *Thomas the Train's* narrator would have been if he didn't have his own self-governor. The thing to remember is that your governor shouldn't be the driver of your words and actions—it should only be there to keep the compass moving in the right direction. When we are trying to be too professional, the governor is usually doing the driving, and when the governor is doing the driving, we aren't really being ourselves.

Too many times we navigate through sales calls or any type of personal interaction driven by our conscious minds. The little governor's voice inside us that intercepts every thought that comes from our brains before it spills out of our mouth. It ensures that we speak eloquently and in a most "professional" manner, reducing our potential level of embarrassment. Not causing embarrassment is a good thing. The question is, why do we fail to trust our true thoughts, and why do we enable this little voice to audit our real personalities? In all actuality, the other person with whom we are conversing with would probably find your true thoughts much more interesting and memorable. Quite frankly, the essence of who we are has been compromised by the changing culture in which we now live. Unfortunately, this once little governor we all have keeps growing stronger and louder as we become more and more sensitive to what is "politically correct" these days. So much so that our personalities, the things that make us shine, become suffocated.

Selling the Unexpected

The only way to respond to the unexpected is to listen. Hearing is not the same thing as listening. A response from hearing is like giving rote responses to anything your significant other says. "Honey, did you take out the trash?" "Yeah, yeah." "Did you fix the stump?" "Yeah, yeah." "I am having an affair with the mailman." "Yeah, ok, honey I'll pick up some OJ on the way home." She knows you're not listening to her, and she gets the proof when she confesses that she's having an affair with the mailman, which she will do if her husband doesn't start *listening*.

My wife and I have been perfecting the art of mind reading for our act. What we do is perfectly natural—it's part of being human—we tirelessly worked to access this part of our humanity that is lost in ten million voices throughout the day that demand every person's attention.

In our show, I venture into the crowd looking for volunteers who will let me look into their pocket, purses or wallets while blindfolded from the stage, while my wife describes exactly what I am seeing. She can even recite the serial number of a dollar bill from across the room. This is impressive, and it should be, but it's a delicate practice that requires a favorable environment. If you can't fly a kite in a thunderstorm, I can't practice mind reading with 40,000 stereos blasting in my head (if you're thinking about seeing some awesome mind reading, don't bring your AC/DC - *For Those About to Rock*).

All that being said: it's more probable that we'll fail than succeed because the listening is so extremely delicate. Sometimes the environment is so good that we can enjoy a long effect, involving the crowd, and everyone is able to enjoy the wonder and possibility of real magic. About half the time, the environment just isn't conducive and we need to improvise.

Fortunately, we don't need to read anyone's mind to work our magic in a sales environment. And even if we could, would we really want to? Mind reading has taken away some of the fun of the holidays in our house: wrapping paper is no longer a necessity at Christmas, and it no longer makes sense to hide eggs at Easter.

Anything can happen during a sales call. Well, not anything, but it will surprise you. When the unexpected happens, a sales magician has prepared so well that s/he can use the unexpected to their advantage. You may walk into a hostile room where the buyers have just had a heated argument and are angry, they could be disappointed from a rough quarterly review, or they could simply be frustrated with each other because of their conflicting personalities. Someone might be asking inane, useless, or senseless questions. Someone on the team might be a heckler. The important thing to remember is you cannot control what other people do, but you can only respond appropriately if you are listening. Everything that happens must become part of the show.

Years ago, one of my specialties was performing at halftime shows for professional sports teams. This has included basketball, hockey, and arena football. My team and I performed at countless halftime shows, once at Madison Square Garden. It is incredibly difficult for a magician to misdirect thousands of people who are viewing the magician from all sides. Usually, magicians have some kind of cover; for example, no one is looking behind them at all times. Most effects are designed with the assumption that the magician is only being viewed by one perspective rather than being completely surrounded by people.

Performing for thousands of people is quite different from a sales pitch, but the secrets for success are exactly the same. Instead of determining the personality types of the few people in the room and asking leading questions, I had to choose a small section of the arena and use their reactions as a springboard for misdirecting the entire crowd. Long before the performance, I read, studied, and performed my effects by myself and with my team until the effect was flawless. We had our performance time cut down to the second because the game was on live TV with paid-for commercial airtime—there's not much room for recovery. We had to instantly capture an audience and convince them that we could do the impossible. I'm not going to lie here—having a staff full of beautiful girls went a long way to help with earning the attention of the audience and misdirecting them. We prepared for the unexpected, and the unexpected happened.

Once we were performing an illusion called *Tilted Trapeziod* where I uncovered a custom made 9-foot tall plexiglass trapezoid. Then, I blew up a balloon and let the audience bounce it around a bit. When the balloon got back to me, I'd pop it and a white dove would instantly appear in its place. Next, I locked the dove on a perch in the trapezoid. I'd do my magician bit—cover the contraption, spin it around, uncover it, and a girl would appear in the trapezoid. In one performance, the dove escaped before I popped the balloon and flew a couple hundred feet high into the rafters of the arena where we were performing. The only thing I could do was smile and provides a "ta-da!" type gesture towards the dove as it flew away. The crowd laughed hysterically. Unfortunately, we never recovered the bird. In a more memorable performance, we couldn't get one of the girls out of the trapezoid because the lock was stuck. I don't think that anyone noticed that anything was wrong. I could tell that the girl was a little worried, but after the show we were able to cut the lock and get her out. No one in the crowd knew any better. For all they knew, the girl was supposed to continue dancing around in the box for the rest of the show. These could have been some embarrassing moments, but because I earned the audience's participation in the effect, I was able to control myself and the effect despite an unforeseen situation.

Sometimes you'll misread a person's personality and what they want from you—what they need for a personal connection. The key is to get good enough at reading the room that you make the right assessment the first time, but you never know what's going to happen. That's one of the things that make sales so much fun.

In magic, the effect from the illusion is going to work if you practice it enough, but connecting with the audience on a personal level and leading them through the effect makes it magical.

The Cardinal Rule

The magic community is a secretive bunch. If you know anything about magic, you've probably heard your new cardinal rule: *A magician never reveals his or her secrets.* Once the secrets are out, it's over. There's no illusion, no captivation, no fun. Imagine learning that Santa Claus isn't 'real.' This usually happens at school, where older children mix with younger children, and the older kids like to see the reaction of the younger kids when the window is shattered. Learning about the 'reality' of Santa takes the first little bit of magic out of Christmas. Once the secret is discovered, the magic is lost.

So everything about magic is impossible for outsiders to learn, and it's difficult for a student to learn. Magic is a secret society, almost like the Masons in the sense that the only people who reveal the secrets either (1) never knew anything in the first place or (2) are disgruntled with the community and want to cause it harm or (3) their greed kicks in and financial reward for unethical practice takes over. When secrets are revealed, one must consider the source. There are magicians who debunk classic and contemporary effects, robbing people of an experience with magic.

We will be skirting the edge of the cardinal rule in this book. The secrets of magic will be revealed because they can improve your life. You will learn five secrets of magic that are behind the successful performance of a magic effect. If you want to learn more secrets, you will have to become a registered member of the family.

Chapter 2 Recap

- Listening is asking leading questions
- Ask what they do and how did they get there
- Use the unexpected to your advantage

Magic for Thought

1. What is your favorite leading question?

2. What are three leading questions specific to your product that you need to ask in the course of every call?

3. How well do you function when the unexpected happens?

The world is full of magic things, patiently waiting for our senses to grow sharper.

W. B. Yeats

Chapter 3

Mastering the Basics

Animating the Plan
Guiding the Sales Call
Involving Your Partner
Casting Your Spell

The first secret of the MAGIC method is *Mastering the Basics*. We've been covering some of the basics already, and in this chapter we'll take a look at the secret of mastering them. In chapter one, we covered the three pillars of the MAGIC method: reading, study, and preparation. Now we'll talk about what you need to read, what it means to study, and the benefits of preparation. Chapter two addressed more basic topics: asking leading questions and what it takes to make a lasting impression. Please remember that I'm not setting out the secrets of magic so you can sell effortlessly. Like a good magician, you will be able to make sales *appear* effortless.

This book is intended to inspire you to keep reading and never, never stop. Study means coming back to this book again and again—and all your important books—gleaning more insight into the method from your experience. Preparation means practicing your craft to perfection so you can perform under pressure. Now we'll apply these principles to using gestures, building indestructible relationships, walking in your competitor's shoes, and mastering your preparation.

What We Say with Our Gestures

There are a lot of books specifically geared towards body language that can shed a tremendous amount of light on this important aspect of selling. Professional poker players know the power of gesture. That's why we see them on TV wearing dark sunglasses, trying to remain completely incognito. These poker players are masters of human gesture, at least when it comes to cards. What are they watching for? The following chart presents some basic gestures that you should pick up on during a sales call.

Speaking with Gestures

Gesture	Meaning	Your Response
Crossed arms or legs	Closed off / Not open to suggestion	Be inviting
Eyes up and to the right	Pensive / thinking	You've got their attention
Touch nose	Something stinks	Earn trust
Rub chin	Interested	Ask a confirmation question i.e., "Does that make sense to you?"
Touch pinkie finger	Indicates stress	Make sure you are not building pressure
Touch ring finger	Emotional (positive)	Ask a confirmation question i.e., "Tell me about your concerns"
Touch middle finger	Anger	Slow down and earn trust
Touch pointer finger	Fear	Earn trust
Lean in	Interested	Ask a confirmation question i.e., "What is your opinion?"
Backing away	Lacking interest	Ask more probing questions, find mutual ground again
Touching a watch	Hurry up	Advance the call
Looking behind you	Losing interest	Advance the call
Casual nodding up and down	agreement or hurry up and finish	Ask a confirmation question i.e., "How does that sound to you?"

The chart above is a general guide, the bare minimum of what you need to know to avoid common pitfalls and read basic gestures. The exact meaning will vary from person to person according to their personality type, but I've found that these gestures are fairly reliable. You can test yourself—when you touch your nose while watching the news or talking with someone, are you indicating mistrust? How many times have you pointed with your index finger at the TV (usually followed by a long string of expletives) because of something like a bad call in a football game? Watch yourself and those around you—when their arms are crossed, are they disinterested? The professional card players we discussed delve into this much deeper. Would you believe that they hone their detection mechanics so precisely that they watch facial micro-expressions, breathing patterns, moisture build up on the face, and pupil dilation? Not only can this help us determine what someone else is thinking, but also what you're conveying to others with your own gestures.

We need to watch what we're saying to the customer with our gestures. These interpretations are fairly common, so it's not out of the question for a customer to read your gestures.

We never want to cross our arms or legs to indicate an unwillingness to communicate. We obviously should never be chewing on our fingernails—it's a surefire way to communicate fear or anger (or both), depending on what finger we're gnawing on. So we should continually check ourselves, because our customers and competitors are paying attention.

We always, always, always look the customer in the eye. It's a simple thing that really should go without saying but if we pay attention, we might be surprised how many times we find ourselves struggling to maintain eye contact with someone during a conversation. Our customers will see our honesty and sincerity. One way to ensure we are doing this effectively is to try to remember all of our customer's eye colors. If we can rattle off all of our customer's eye colors, we know that we have been practicing great eye contact. When you look your customer in the eye and tell them what they will get from your product, you are on your way to cultivating the connection for the kind of relationship that you need.

We should never underestimate the power of eye contact. The eye is the window to the soul, and there's something humanizing about the eye-to-eye connection. A few years ago, my wife and I had a difficult time trying to get our three-year-old son's attention when he was acting up. We'd call him by name and he would just merrily go on playing in the toilet. But we started saying, "Trent. Look at me." He'd stop, look us in the eye, and we could temporarily keep him from setting the house on fire. One day I was at my desk, and Trent wanted a toy that he couldn't reach. I could barely hear him, and I just kept putting it off because I didn't want to stop whatever it was that I was doing. I then heard my name. "Da-da! Look at me!" I was horrified at what I might see. Last time he said something like this, he had two handfuls of his own poo and wanted me to see him smear it on the wall. I spun my chair around to look my son in the eye, and in beautiful three-year-old English he said, "Now that I have your attention, please get that toy!" Eye contact works.

Disclaimer: If we're going to use gestures to inform ourselves during our sales calls, we need to be sure to memorize them correctly. We don't want to be the salesperson that misreads a customer and makes it worse by responding inappropriately. Now that we're armed and ready, we can practice reading ourselves and our significant others, friends, and co-workers. There are a lot of books specifically geared towards body language that can shed a tremendous amount of light on this important aspect of selling. When we've mastered our gestures, we can use that as one of the tools to build indestructible relationships.

Building Indestructible Relationships

We must develop indestructible relationships with our customers. When we do this, we'll be able to learn how our competitors are selling. What are they telling our current and potential customers about their products? When we invest in our customers and build indestructible relationships, they will do some of your homework for you. Our competitors will contact our customers eventually, and if we have built indestructible relationships with our customers, they will call us and spill the beans. We'll have a good laugh at all the silly stuff that the "other guy" is doing, and our friend will tell us exactly how to exploit our competitors' weaknesses.

This is how I found out about suits. I am in medical sales, and I had suited up—hardcore—every day of my sales career until a customer called me and told me about a meeting he'd just had with a few salesmen. Never mind the product, the sales team (three gentlemen) lost the sale before they even sat down. They were dressed to the nines, and every one of them shook his hand. All three of them. They lost the customer's trust and could never earn it back, because the gentlemen had an arrogant tone that comes with it. My friend said, "As I looked across my desk, each one of them looked slicker than the next." This isn't bad on Wall Street, and maybe this is where these guys belonged, but in sales we need to be able to connect with real people in real situations. We can't pretend to be somewhere else—and more importantly—someone we're not.

On the suits: in the medical profession, all of the clinicians wear scrubs. That is, everyone who is in the "in" crowd: the nurses, doctors, and surgeons who are doing the work of medicine. Administrators still come to work in suits, but they are usually sequestered in their offices, and they usually aren't the folks that I sell to (but when I do, I wear a suit). Anyway, my friend was in his scrubs after a morning of surgery, and these three suits walk in pretending to know everything. My friend couldn't connect with these gentlemen because they looked "slick." They were more like hospital administrators than hospital workers, even in the high-end surgical suites.

So I took a cue from my friend and bought some scrubs. All of the sudden I was prom queen. When I ate in the cafeteria, people sat with me and talked, and wanted to take me out to lunch sometime. People were instantly open and honest with me! Suddenly I was a natural, like the salesperson that people want to buy from before a word is spoken. I was the most interesting man in the world. When I was wearing a suit, this never happened. I had to sit at the kids' table, a social pariah playing Pee Wee Herman to my Conan O'Brien.

Remember when I said that my friend was put off by the handshaking? It's perfectly fine to give a sincere handshake to the customer in most situations. But there's a hand sanitizer bolted to the outside of the man's door. He's a surgeon, and those hand sanitizers are outside and inside every door in the hospital. He probably sanitizes his hands a thousand times a day, and he remembers that the soap dries out his hands because they lack a strong enough moisturizer. *Dried out a surgeon's hands.* When the salesmen walked into his office and shook his hand, they were practically yelling at the top of their lungs that they knew nothing about the inconveniences of his business, *even if in fact they were quite knowledgeable.* Thanks, guys! I am reminded to always use those hand sanitizers myself, a tiny detail that speaks volumes about my character and the effort I take to learn my market.

In sales, the last thing we want to do is some little thing that shuts off our customer. Sometimes there's no recovery, as with the case described above. If we read up and study our market—and listen to our customers when they tell us about other salespeople, we'll be improving our sales using the secrets of magic.

Walk a Mile in Your Competitors' Shoes

Our customers will sometimes tell us what the competition is doing. Even so, we need to imagine how our competitor is selling their product—and more importantly—how they are exploiting our weaknesses. While our customers' opinions are invaluable, we will need to do most of our own recon. I start by getting ahold of one of my competitor's products, and figuring out how I would sell it.

To walk in our competitors' shoes, we can role-play a sales call with our spouses or colleagues, taking turns playing salesperson and customer—with both our product and all of our competitors' products. It's actually a lot of fun, and we can work while spending a little quality time with our family or friends. This method is extremely effective. The pros know it— huge corporations pay big money for role-playing seminars so their sales teams can get inside everyone's heads: the customer, the competition, and themselves. As we're role-playing, we need to find the good in our products and truly believe that we're the "good guys and girls." We can be 100% certain that our competitors know the good things about their product and believe that they are the "good girls and guys." If they know what they are doing, and often they do, they will know the basics, too, and they will be using the basics to the best of their ability. This we should always remember, because however much we forget this, our competitor earns exponentially more in market share.

As we are preparing, we will not neglect the "little guy and girl." We need to consider the "little girl and guy" as worthy competition and prepare for them just as much as we prepare for the bullies.   Consider that it's easier to get to the top than to stay on top, and the big dogs of today most likely will not be the major players in the future.   Years ago, everyone had a Blackberry—it was the best phone on the market.   Now, they are falling behind tremendously; they have a loyal customer base, but they are unable to innovate fast enough to compete. In sales, it's not what you've done in the past that matters; it's what you are doing tomorrow. We want lasting success, so we don't want anyone challenging our market share.

The "little girl or guy" has nothing to lose. Hopefully, this isn't you right now, and the simple fact that you're reading this book indicates that you're probably not. In any case, the "little guy or girl" might be in a small startup in which s/he might be the only salesperson / bookkeeper / marketer / everything else. This poor guy/lady might be working an 80hr week, honestly trying to make a living. However, the "little guy or girl" might be peddling an inferior product for a company that has a tiny market share in your primary market. In my field, it's possible for a medical device company to fund a clinical trial, pay doctors and hospitals to participate, and give their product away as a bonus. Recent regulations have prevented companies from even giving away pens with their logos on it, so it's not so simple as I've described, but I compete with people who are giving products away and paying customers to take it. How do I compete with this "little guy or girl"? Simple: I am an honest salesperson who is selling a product that benefits my customers far more than me, and honest customers—the ones I want as indestructible relationships—know better than to participate in illegal activities.

If we know our product well and communicate to our customers that our product meets a genuine need, our customers can easily distinguish us from the salespeople who are trying to make a quick buck. When I go to a medical conference or trade show, my friends and I can easily spot the new companies. They are the ones handing out goodies, sponsoring raffles for vacations, and otherwise trying to illegally woo hospitals and doctors. I assume that these companies simply didn't bother to learn their new market (at best), or are exploiting what little time they have to penetrate the market by cheating the system. The lesson here: the "little guy/lady" may be peddling a product that they may not understand in a market that they don't understand. But they can and will leap out of the woodwork and enjoy a meteoric rise to the top if you cannot anticipate their next move. Whoever the "little guy/girl" is, they are always hungry, and if you allow them to steal any of your customers, it will benefit them far more than you will lose. Any gain in market share is a gigantic shot in the arm for them, and they will gain more market share from a single customer and become a fat cat in the blink of an eye.

Our advantage is that we have mastered everything related to our market. We know what we need to wear, how we need to speak, and what mannerisms we should assume, because we have read up on our market and we listen to our customers. We have imagined and role-played how our competitors sell. We know what they are saying about their product, and we know if this is true because we know their product.

One invaluable thing that an indestructible relationship produces is letters of reference. I happened to work with an old purchasing director at Yale New Haven Hospital, who has since moved on. When I told him that I was thinking about transitioning to another company, he wrote a glowing letter of recommendation for me, and his influence was extremely helpful. At the time, I couldn't believe it, a sales guy getting a letter of recommendation from a purchasing director of a very well-respected institution. Then I realized, I worked very hard at building that relationship and an indestructible relationship will allow you to use them as references. I can't tell you how many times this has happened while performing magic as well. Many of my customers have offered to have new potential customers call them at any time. Obviously, I always call first to give the heads up, and they have come through for me time and time again.

Some times an indestructible relationship will afford us opportunity to evaluate a new product for us before we launch into the market. It's a wonderful advantage to find out how the product performs in the real world with friends before we sell to new customers. We might find that the product has advantages that were previously unknown to us, or we could discover that the product needs some additional development. In addition to this, they give us new ideas for new products that will make their jobs easier. As a magician, I contact my old customers to see if I can stop by and try out new effects with them. This enables me to get in front of a well-tailored audience for my new material while studying feedback. It also enables me to talk about future booking opportunities.

Indestructible relationships are well worth our time and effort. Most of this time and effort is simply investing in people. Just as not every sale will close, most of the people that we get to know will not produce one of these wonderful relationships that I've described. We can learn to identify people who will be advocates for us, but nothing beats the feeling of a customer calling us out of the blue, bragging about how they just gave a good reference for us and the number of the potential customer. Or the customer who calls and tells us what the competition is up to. That's priceless, and that's why we bend over backwards for our customers. Happy customers produce more customers who are more likely to close.

Mastering Your Preparation

If it sounds like I'm repeating myself, it's because this point is very important. Sometimes a salesperson is born—a natural — but most salespersons are made. No one is born a magician— all magicians are made.

No one is born with a natural disposition for performing a magic trick like *cups and balls*. When a magician performs this effect well, you now know that he or she read, practiced, and studied work up to the point of guiding perfect strangers through a complex effect. Mastering the basics is about learning the basic techniques, but if the magician gets distracted by showing off the basic flourishes and false transfers, people will focus on the small stuff and everyone will miss the beauty of the trick. Unlike the magicians, some salespeople are born.

A natural salesperson is like a Golden Retriever puppy, and has a natural advantage in every sales call. This puppy is the quintessential people person, but not just a people person, a people winner. People want to be the puppy's friend, love the puppy, and buy whatever the puppy is selling. It's sort of like me in my scrubs—but I wasn't born with them, I was practically told to get them by a customer.

Most salespeople started out as Ug, the ugliest dog in the world. I mean this from the bottom of my heart. This was me without my scrubs. Nobody wants to snuggle up to Ug, like everyone seems suspicious of the suit. Cute women in scrubs looked right through my suit to the buck-toothed guy in scrubs. The doctors that buy from me don't want to be near a suit; they are irritated by an ignorant someone who wants to correct them, tell them that they are using an inferior product, and otherwise frustrate them.

When a salesperson masters the basics, Ug is dressed to kill as a yellow Labrador puppy. No body complains about snuggling up to a yellow Lab, wishing instead that it is a Golden. Most people can't even tell the difference between a yellow Lab and a Golden, especially when they are puppies. Both are yellow, soft, fluffy, curious, and almost exactly the same build and temperament. Fortunately for the rest of us, natural salespeople are uncommon, and customers can't tell the difference between a natural and a well-trained salesperson. That's why most of us have jobs. I mention this rare bird only because most salespeople who think they are naturals actually need to learn something about sales, and can benefit from the simple tap on the shoulder from a good-natured salesperson saying, "This has worked for me, and I think it can work for you." Even a Golden might cock her head to the side to listen to the secrets of a yellow Lab's success.

So how does Ug (the ugliest dog in the world) transform into a yellow Lab puppy? Why, by dressing up like a Golden by practicing the MAGIC method. All magicians begin without advantage; it's an even playing field. There are no Golden magicians—all master magicians are yellow Labs. The first secret of magic is that a good magician became good because of a commitment to practice. After *mastering the basics,* it's time to breathe life into the sales call by *animating the plan*

Chapter 3 Recap

- What you and your customer say with gestures

- The power of indestructible relationships

- Know your competition through role-play

- Magicians aren't born, they practice

Magic for Thought

1. What can you know about what's going on in your customer's head by watching their gestures?

2. What can you do to develop and nurture indestructible relationships?

3. How have you helped out another salesperson by being their indestructible ally?

The magic is there, even when we know the secrets.

Chapter 4

Mastering the Basics

Animating the Plan

Guiding the Sales Call

Involving Your Partner

Casting Your Spell

Do you want to live like Houdini?

Now that we have *mastered the basics*, it's time to *animate the plan*. We need to breathe life into our preparation. When a magician performs *cups and balls*, it cannot be a rote repetition of a set of instructions. The effect has to have life. It can't be a replication of what happened in practice or something that worked in the past. In order to have life, there must be something fresh and new about the performance—the magician has to be responsive to the audience in order to effectively guide them through the effect.

We're not simply reading, studying, and preparing, expecting all of this to come together without effort. The point of the MAGIC method is to give a high level of energy and vitality to your entire sales performance. We've learned that the first secret of magic is that magicians aren't born, they are made through diligent preparation. Magicians appear to make the impossible happen because no one can see all of the hard work that brings everything together to create a dazzling effect. No one is born with the ability to mix up a deck of cards and begin to instantly create awe-inspiring, wonderful effects— everyone has to seek out the secrets of the effect and practice relentlessly. One of the reasons why magicians are successful is that their preparation and execution are animated: the plan is a living, organic thing that captivates the human mind.

Talk to the Right Person

Your plan is completely lifeless if you don't know how to find the right person to talk to. The best thing to do is get a good view of the landscape before you begin. You need to know your market, who the decision makers are, and how to best reach these people. You don't want all of your hard work to be wasted on a useless sales call because the person you're talking to isn't the one who can choose to buy. I have been guilty of this before. We're looking for Aces and Kings.

In my field, there are many decision makers. I'm selling products that could cost the hospital hundreds of thousands of dollars over a number of years, and I've made deals for a lot more. There are a lot of hands in the cookie jar: clinicians, purchasing agents, clinical educators, risk managers, and materials managers. In my early days, I tried to chase down decision makers one at a time. I wish I could get all that energy back! I have found that if I get a key hospital employee excited about my product, they would assist me by orchestrating some of the meetings for me. Once they could visualize the advantages for the product (i.e., it made their job easier, was better clinically for their patients or it was monetarily better in some fashion) they were always more than happy to become an apostle, one who would round the troops and bring the fanfare. So instead of locating and wooing a dozen people, I simply looked for a head nurse and made her an apostle for my product. She would help me tremendously by going around selling the product to the doctors and administrators, and I could focus on preparing my presentation to an entire committee once she helped gather everyone on board. Spies used to do this kind of thing—create operatives to do their bidding back on the operative's home soil. It's brilliant.

Positioning

As we're doing our research, we need to determine how we're going to position ourselves. Understanding where we are in the market is tricky sometimes because the rules are always changing. Obviously, we don't want to position ourselves as a power player if we happen to be a startup. You don't want to pretend to be backed up with the same kind of research and reputation of a major corporation if you are outdone by all your competitors. Positioning needs to match the nature of our company and our product. We are an extension of our products, so we're positioning ourselves at the same time. If we stray too far up or down, we'll lose market share. People want to buy products that are accurately represented.

Good positioning is a powerful tool. One of the businesses my family and I started was an Italian ice company that we named after my daughter Emilee. We initially marketed ourselves as what we were: a small family-run business. When we approached grocery stores with our product, we went there together as a family and built good relationships with the mom and pop businesses. Our approach worked wonderfully because we had our family face front and center. Our brand grew and became well recognized in the region. We were able to expand and began selling to professional baseball stadiums when suddenly, the big dogs ate our lunch. Almost instantly, we were treated like major national distributors who were lining the owners' pockets with all kinds of incentives that we couldn't afford to give as a small family business. So we learned that our positioning worked powerfully in one market, but melted quickly in another.

Proper positioning gives life to your sales calls. If you know yourself and your product's position in the market, you can effectively present it within its own context. This is important, because if you don't know your position, you look like you don't know what you're talking about. You are avoiding this situation now because you've already done your homework about your product and all of your competitors' products, so you know how you best fit within this landscape. Your customer probably knows this, too, so they aren't going to be fooled by attempts to make your product look like something it's not. It is very embarrassing to lose a sale because you oversold or undersold your product.

Finally, animating your plan includes understanding what type of sale you are pitching. The type of sale you are working on can typically be identified as either a product or solution sale. The solution sale is much more complex and is ordinarily driven at a slower speed. Are you selling a commodity type item or something that is a large ticket item? Is this sale a quick close up magic or a longer full-scale illusion show? Are you selling used cars or high tech? Is what you are selling a one stop sales call or is it going to be a much longer process compiled of many sales meetings? Be honest: although the money would be nice, is it realistic to get a sale today? Or is it worth waiting, adding to your pipeline and coming back later when the time is more appropriate?

Role-Play: The Elevator Pitch

We talked before about the value of role-play. The elevator pitch is an outstanding way to practice your sales calls. This isn't a new idea. We should be able to deliver our sales pitch in 30 seconds, consisting of the key drivers of our product. This is what movie producers do in the trailers they use to market their movies. They build up an entire movie in 30 seconds that they hope will inspire us to go see it. Now, I don't mean speaking so fast that our customer has no idea what we're saying. In role-play, we work our pitch down to 30 seconds. If our friends don't get it in that amount of time, we need to make adjustments until they do, practicing over and over again. By the time we actually make the sales call, we'll have memorized the most important components of our pitch, and we'll be able to temper the temptation to destroy our sale through gab. We don't want to fall on our own sword, prattling on about stuff that our client cares less about, and lose their attention rather than captivating him/her with our colorful personality.

Consulting vs. Selling

Consulting with our customer breathes life into our sales calls. We shouldn't be learning how to be so slick that we entice our customer to close. People can see right through that unless you're a sales god/goddess. Most salespeople who arrogantly try to tell the customer what they need, that their product is what they need, and aggressively try to close the deal don't last very long in the business. Good sales is built on positive relationships that are guided by the salesperson's commitment to consulting the customer.

When we've internalized all of this stuff, we transform from salespersons to consultants—product pitchers to partners. I have customers who call me and say, "Chris, this is our situation. What can you do for us?" I can talk to them about how my products will meet their needs. I'm not perceived as always delivering a sales pitch. I am consulting with my clients, advising them how to best meet their need. Consulting is far more rewarding than sales. It's customer driven, and they love it. If we can communicate to our customers that we put their needs first, explaining how our product works to this end, we're no longer salespersons but consultants. As consultants, we resolve issues that trigger emotional concerns—remember *effect* vs. *trick*—we become experts at finding solutions. By concentrating on becoming an advisor, we begin to eliminate the feeling people get from salespeople of "being sold."

Smile with Passion

We talked earlier about laughing with the customer no matter what. This is just part of sales. We laugh with our customers. But we need to ensure we are giving our smile some passion; we need to be genuine. This isn't easy for everyone at first, but once you make it a way of life, it's a piece of cake. More importantly than that, smiling can change your life. Truly smiling.

Smiles are powerful. Recently I was Christmas shopping at the mall and a little kid caught my attention. She had to be four or five years old, and she was unhappy. Very unhappy. One might even say that she was irate. Her grandmother was ready to go, and her little granddaughter had her best frown on, arms crossed, and heels firmly dug in. Grandma smiled and patiently walked up to her and said something like this: "Come on, I know that there's a smile in there somewhere." The little girl continued to try to maintain her frown, but just couldn't resist her grandmother's prompts. I could see the frown slowly morph into a smile. She turned around, and the smiling Grandma said, "My little girl has a smile on her face. Now let's go..." The grandmother's smile had passion. There was something behind the smile that animated it, that gave it life. When she spoke, I could hear the smile.

Our smiles must be animated. We really should be having fun! The lifeless smile of the salesman is a nail in the coffin of his/her career. We need to learn how to laugh with our customers no matter what. The customer is not going to be fooled by a laugh that is too forced or badly timed. They will be laughing at themselves, and we need to learn how to laugh with them. The best way to learn to smile is through practice—doing it all the time even on the phone. We can watch the dynamic of a conversation change just by smiling while we talk on the phone. I recently read that smiling actually changes the tone of your voice to a more pleasant octave.

Chapter 4 Recap

- Breathe life into your call
- Look for Aces and Kings
- Position yourself and your product
- Pitch the elevator
- Consult, don't sell
- Smile with passion
- Know when to move to the next step in the system

Magic for Thought

How well do your competitors position their products?

Are you comfortable seeing yourself as a consultant?

How would your sales pitch change if you viewed yourself as an extension of your product?

Magic is believing in yourself, if you can do that, you can make anything happen.

Johann Wolfgang von Goethe

Chapter 5

Mastering the Basics

Animating the Plan

Guiding the Sales Call

Involving your Partner

Casting Your Spell

How to capture an audience like Houdini

Houdini gave people incredible experiences that they would never forget. He seemed to have a superhuman ability to escape from all manner of locks and restraints, often underwater or hanging 10 stories upside down in the air. A show was a success if people were entertained and managing to get Houdini out alive was a secondary concern. As we're guiding the call, we are taking people from wherever they started to where we want them to be. Before we came into their lives, they might not have given a second thought to the need that our product addresses better than anything else. It's our task to guide the call so that the customer is comfortable with choosing us. The vehicle that will get us there is the leading question. As we said before, the customer needs to arrive to the decision to buy on their own—it has to be their idea—so the leading questions allow the customer to explore their need for the product and how it will benefit their business. This process must be invisible to the customer—if your customer can see right through you, they no longer own their decision-making process.

Five Card Connection

Guiding the sales call should be a smooth, natural process. The objective is to craft the conversation so that the customer owns the decision to close. Any influence that we have over the conversation—guiding the customer to realize how badly they need what we're selling, focusing on how our products meet their needs, and making our product invaluable—must be invisible.

Let's try a little experiment. On the outside back cover of this book there are some playing cards. In a moment, I am going to ask you to select one, but not yet. First, I want you to just familiarize yourself with them. Please take a peek at the cards.

You'll notice that there are five cards. Before you select one, you may be thinking that I am trying to influence you somehow.

For instance, I may have placed the *King of Hearts* in the group because it's the only picture card and it may stand out more than the others; therefore, you may select it. Likewise, the *Seven of Clubs* may influence your decision because it's the only black card. Or maybe the *Ace of Diamonds* is there because it's the highest card in the group.

I could probably rattle off a number of reasons for each card, on why they may be possible influencers. Please don't let these things impact your decision.

Now, take another peek and select one in your mind. Focus on that card for a moment.

Did you think of the *Nine of Diamonds*? If so, that doesn't surprise me because typically about 20% of the people choose that card just by chance.

However, there is something even more surprising. 50% of the people usually choose the card on the front cover of the book. Now look very closely. If that was your card – was it probability or was the power of suggestion used here?

Did you see the *Four of Hearts* there?

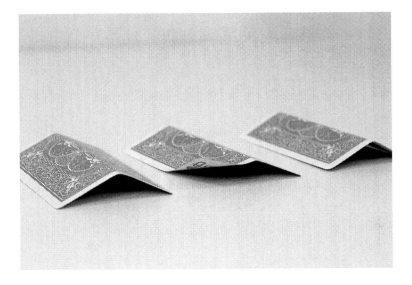

Three Card Monte

This can be an enjoyable effect for the performer and at the same time a real mindscrambler for the audience. This effect can be presented as a wonderful display of entertainment or a way to scam an innocent victim out of hard earned money.

Similar to the cups and balls, there are three cards. The object is to follow the Queen of Hearts as the dealer skillfully tosses the cards around face down. The observers learn quickly that this game of chance leaves them absolutely no chance, even when the dealer "accidentally" bends the corner of the Queen.

In the *cups and balls* trick, you've just got them going. You're piquing their interest, allowing them to see just a little and want a little more. This is the heart of the effect, when the crowd becomes fully engaged in the narrative.

The *Three Card Monte* card game illustrates this concept well. Hustlers have used this game for longer than I know, and it's still in use today. Magicians use it for entertaining because the trick is so reliable that no one will ever pick the right card - which is why it's a sure bet for hustlers. The dealer shows three cards, one of which is the *Queen of Hearts*. All three cards have a crease in the middle of the back so they can stand face down. The dealer mixes the cards and invites the onlookers to bet on which card is the Queen. The dealer does a few demonstrations, showing how easy it is to choose the Queen. He or she will then bend the corner of the card (seemingly by accident) to make it appear like a sure bet. A buddy of the dealer's will then place the first bet and win. After that, onlookers might place a small bet and the hustler will let them win until a more substantial bet is made. It works every time, provided the hustler knows what s/he is doing, and frankly, I have never seen it *not* work. The *guide the call* component is when the onlookers get drawn into the excitement of the trick: when they are watching the demonstrations and view it as the hustler desires: it's a harmless card game in which they have more than a sure chance of winning.

What Problems Can We Solve?

During this stage of the call, we're discovering how exactly our product fits within the customer's perception of their needs. There will always be something about our product that works better than anything else in the market. In fact, there might be a lot of things about our product that makes it stand out. As we ask our probing questions, we will be listening for how we can best position our product according to what our customer wants and needs, listening for that one thing or set of things that our product can do exceptionally well. We'll be taking notes and identifying three or four major issues that our product can solve.

When I'm performing magic, I am constantly interacting with my audience. I almost always need a little bit of information to work with, and if it's good, I can exploit it for the rest of the show. Now I've been doing this for a while, so I can work just about anything into an effect, weaving the audience into the show. I can also create participation by tossing something into the crowd, like a deck of cards—then have a few people select cards, and have the magic happen right there in their hands. I could have performed the effect on stage with an assistant, but I'd be the only one doing the magic. I build ownership throughout my show, inviting the audience to invest in it, and the more involved they are, the more impact my show will have.

In my other life, as you know well by now, I sell medical devices, so my initial questions go something like this:

- What do you currently use in the facility?
- Is there any resistance to change from your staff? [or anyone else, depending on the situation]
- If you could change one or two things about your product, what would that be?
- What do you really like about your current product?

Then, I dig a little deeper, asking questions in logical order so the customer can conclude that my product is the best solution:

118

- How do those one or two things that you would like to change, if you could, effect your overall productivity on a daily, monthly, yearly basis?
- How does this affect your staff?
- Do you think it affects the morale, productivity and/or their job satisfaction level?
- If you were to all it all up, what do you think the overall cost factor to your organization's bottom line is?

Because I've done my research, I already know how badly the hospital needs my product. So the customer is feeding me information that I already know... the point is that they are admitting to themselves that their current situation is not ideal, and I'm taking them down the logical path that I'm setting up through my questions. I'm searching for the one little gem that will make me look like an absolute wizard.

About Price

I've already noted that a typical rookie mistake is pulling out your product in the beginning of the call. When this happens, the customer is only interested in the product and has no interest in how we are positioning it to meet their needs.

It's the same way with price. Customers are always interested in price, and sometimes they will be a little aggressive with it. However, we don't want to reveal price until we've made our product invaluable to them. For me, it's when I see that the customer has fully embraced how much my product will help them. Price is no longer an issue because they know that their current setup costs the hospital a lot more money than my product.

However, if we reveal the price too early, we're done. The negotiation process is over before it has even begun. There are a few ways to address the question in a way that won't kill the sale. First, we'll tell them that we want to find out what products are the best fit for them before we discuss cost. Why would we want to sell something to our customers that really isn't a good fit for them? It's counter productive to our cultivation process. However, if you must give a price, give a price range that helps you. I usually give a wide range, and tell the customer that I can clarify that at a later time, after we've discussed their needs. No matter what our response is, we'll get off the topic of price quickly and focus on the customer's needs.

Why does revealing price early kill the sale? Our customer won't hear anything about how our product will meet their needs if they are distracted by price. As such, we do ourselves our customers a disservice. Our customers won't be informed about our product, and we will loose the sale. This information is critical because the customer has to conclude for him or herself that our product is valuable, and they can't do that if they are distracted by price.

One note on price: the lower the price is, the earlier we can reveal it. In sales situations where we'll never see the customer again, we need to get right to it. Car salespeople face this dilemma on daily basis, and I respect the sales folks who can make a living pushing high-pressure sales. They seem to be the ones caught right in the middle ground between a complex sale and a more simplistic price-based sale. Obviously, this varies depending upon the car manufacturer. A Mercedes salesperson will have a much different approach than someone selling a Prius. The last time I bought a car, I wanted to cut right through all the usual tactics. I understand the drill, and unfortunately for that salesperson, I didn't have time or patience to go through the whole dog and pony show. Don't get me wrong, the mutual respect is there, it just made both of our lives much easier when they were enlightened to the fact that I am in sales as well. I just called them up, told them what I wanted, the price I was willing to pay, they found the car for me, and we closed the deal. No hassle at all, and price was given at the outset. The negotiable variables were reduced to the bells and whistles I wanted with the vehicle.

Listen, Listen, and Listen Some More

As we're *guiding the call*, we'll be listening *far* more than we'll be talking. The act of *guiding the call* doesn't mean that we're talking all the time; we're just giving the conversation a gentle push in the right direction at the right time. The more the customer talks, the more they own the choice to buy, and the more comfortable they'll be to close. At this point, we're letting the sale gain momentum, and that can't happen if we're the stars of the show. So we'll want to keep the worms in the can and leave the opener at home.

Talking too much in sales is like performing one-handed cuts, shuffles, spreads, spinning cards and flourishes in magic. Showcasing these flourishes in the midst of performing for the public is a very bad idea. Sure, it looks fantastic and it boosts the magician's ego, but it indirectly says, *look at what I can do.* In the end, it does nothing to assist the magician's goal of performing miracles. Actually, it can work completely counterproductive to the overall objective. It may be a crowd pleaser for the first few minutes, but beyond that, s/he imbeds the idea in the minds of the spectators that the magician simply has outstanding dexterity with a deck of cards. Anything performed after becomes just a trick or a puzzle with a logical answer in their eyes rather than a miracle.

Remember, we'll be taking notes, listening, and thinking about how to best position our product all at the same time. When we flag a major problem, we'll confirm it and explore it by simply asking, "So I hear that X is really important, tell me more about that." This is especially helpful when we know that our product will solve that problem for them. But as hard as it is, we can't let it on yet; we save it, because we'll have our opportunity.

Revealing the price kills negotiation, and so does talking if we aren't careful. There's an old saying about negotiation that I have found to be true, *the one who talks first loses.* When we reveal price, we're ending the negotiation on price because we've already revealed our hand, even if actual price negotiation comes much later in the call or even later in the sales cycle. The discussions leading up to the closing also have their negotiation components, so the more we say, the more ground we will lose. If we limit our discussion to the qualities of our product that meet their specific needs, and say nothing else other than things that benefit the customer, we're on the right track, and we're getting closer to the harvest.

Chapter 5 Recap

- The customer should realize for himself or herself that your product will solve their problems.
- We hang on to price until the customer is convinced that our product is invaluable
- We guide the call by listening to the customer's needs

Magic for Thought

1. What are some ways that you can practice good listening skills?

2. Have you ever revealed the price too soon?

3. Have you ever purchased a product because it seemed invaluable?

Construct your

miracle.

Chapter 6

Mastering the Basics

Animating the Plan

Guiding the Sales Call

Involving Your Partner

Casting Your Spell

Can we capture the imagination like Houdini?

At this point we should have three or four needs that we can exploit in our pitch. We've already asked a few questions about each point to confirm and evaluate these needs. We may have already known them, but now our customer has admitted them and can own the sales process. Now it's time for the show. Excitement is building and everyone senses that it's leading to the finale. What we do as a salesperson is what every magician hopes for in a show: the audience forgets about the illusion and they are enjoying themselves. They are involved in the effect, and for a moment, magic is real. Customers don't want to own a decision making process that has no life or doesn't impressively solve their problems. The salesperson needs to be more than a salesperson; the product needs to be more than a product. **The salesperson needs to be *their* customer's partner** and the product needs to be *their* customer's solution—before the customer buys anything.

This kind of ownership is essential. Coincidentally, I once saw a group of guys running the *Three Card Monte* swindle on a small group of tourists in New York City. I was very curious to see how good these guys were and what their methodology consisted of, so I stood by and watched from a distance. I was blown away by what I saw. While everyone else only saw the one person running the game, I saw a four-person crew. They were flawless and operated the scam with eloquent precision. They had a crowd of about eight people—one was a family from Kansas or some place. The dad was absolutely confident that he had figured out the game, and the dealer knew it. He was doing everything he needed to do to pull the tourist into his trap, and the dad was already nibbling on the cheese. After the dealer let the tourist guess correctly a few times, an accomplice made the first bet and won. It was technically beautiful, but morally it was an absolute disaster. It was impossible to win, and the dealer took all that guy's money. Once the tourist thought that he owned the game, he was a goner, and the dealer knew it. Time to move in for the kill.

In the much less threatening *cups and balls* effect, the guiding process of the trick has already captured the attention of the audience, and they are beginning to actively participate. They will be guessing where the ball is, while I ask folks where they'd like the ball to be, or pick someone in the audience to guess where the ball is. All the while I work the crowd by making some small talk.

In a sales call, this portion of the call has a dual purpose: helping the customer realize what the issues are with their current product and informing us as to how we can position our product within the framework of their needs and their perception of their needs. The positioning of the product should be perfectly tailored so that the customer wins: they understand your product, they know that their needs will be met, and they estimate that the value of your product is worth far more to them than whatever the price may be.

This last part is extremely critical. Our customer has to have their own very clear understanding of the overall ramifications of their current situation with its costs, damages, and potential for exponential growth without remedy. This positioning might seem like an unattainable ideal, and it will be unless you involve your partner. We need a lot of information from the customer, so our partner needs to be open with us. Fortunately, we'll be asking the right questions, letting our partner talk. The call will be centered completely on our partner, discovering with them their challenges and needs. Buzz words in the conversation will help us determine where our product should be placed with respect to its functionality for the customer, price, and even our partner's buying preferences. Together, these steps allow our partner to own the process and choose to buy from us.

Opening Up

Sometimes the audience doesn't react as a magician would like. In more intimate shows, it's easy to see if the audience is involved in the effect. I can see animated faces, people craning their necks to get a better view, applaud, and laugh when I am waxing hilarious. When I performed at halftime shows, I could still watch a small selection of the crowd to measure audience participation.

When I changed my show from magic effects to mind reading, the cues and gestures that indicated participation changed as well. I quickly noticed that the cheers and clapping switched to questioning looks and silence. We were posed with another challenge. It's a different kind of entertainment, and connecting with the audience at an emotional level required a new approach. I found that the audience was being entertained—people were just knocked out of their socks by the performance and didn't know how to respond. It was also a little intimidating for some people who associate what we do with the supernatural and unexplained phenomena. Instead of relying on audience reactions during the show, we relied on comments after the show. After every mind reading show, people would approach me and ask if we could talk with the dead or invade people's minds. This is *after* I told the audience repeatedly that my wife and I are entertainers and do not dabble in the paranormal or supernatural. Despite all of that, many people still want to believe we can speak to their deceased relatives. Regardless, I can tell we have succeeded in entertaining our audience when we had this type of an effect on people.

We'll find that some people are just impossible for us to read. This is simply a human phenomenon: we don't always understand each other. But because we're complicated beings, we can hide behind all manner of positive or negative emotions and agendas. So we'll begin to doubt ourselves sometimes. If we can't get someone to open up, we won't know if we're asking the right questions and if they are coming to the right conclusions.

Once I had a customer who I could not figure out. I asked him questions, told great jokes, made sure I knew he had brown eyes, and looked at him during key points in the pitch to see if I was getting anywhere. Nothing. During a break I asked around and discovered that we both share the same birthday, Nov. 14. A math whiz will instantly know that Feb. 14 is a very special day for me (assuming a full-term pregnancy). It's worth listing a few other notable birthdays:

- Jan 17 - St. Patrick's Day
- Feb 5 - Cinco de Mayo
- July 31 - Halloween
- July 4 - April Fool's

But nothing is so good as Valentine's Day—it's the best. So I went back into the meeting, made a little joke about birthdays, and the gentleman melted. I didn't mention him at all, but we had something in common and connected. When I won his involvement, he was a goner.

A Customer-Centered Call

The problem needs to be worse than the customer imagined. The customer is going to spend a lot of money on your product, and it needs to solve significant problems and render a significant benefit. So salespersons need to spin the issues to highlight how the product can meet the customer's needs. You need to change into your leotard and cape and become *Captain Solution*—if you can find a phone booth these days. I've already asked my customer about employee morale and productivity, but I haven't addressed more personal issues. I want to show them that there is a discontent in their workforce that can be addressed by my product. I also want to address how my product would benefit their bottom line.

- How frustrated is your staff because of your current product?
- If your current shrinkage continues, how much would that cost the your company over the next five years?
- If you could get rid of that, how would it impact your business?

The bigger the problems are, the more your product is the hero. When my customer really considers the tremendous cost to their business that their current product brings, price is no longer an issue. My product is obviously the best choice: it eases the strain on employees, protects the company's customers, and it's a fraction of the cost of their current setup.

Because I've done my research, I already know how effective their current products are. When I ask questions about their current products, I am listening for cues. Do they know how serious their problem is? Are they honest with themselves about the current situation? Are they even open to talking about this stuff?

As we're delving deeper into these issues, we'll need to be invisible. These questions need to flow out of a conversation that is facilitated by personal connection. The thing is, the people sitting in front of us in all likelihood chose the product that we want them to replace. They don't want to feel like fools now for making a bad choice years ago, and they don't want to make a bad decision about the same thing years later. Depending upon the size of the sale, if they make a bad choice now, it could cost them their reputation or even their career. This is why they need to own their choice to buy, and in order to own it; they need to admit what the issues are. If we're just telling them our assessment of the situation, we're wasting our time. Their assessment is what counts, and our leading questions can help guide this process, but it must be done delicately. In the end, they will be telling us how our product will benefit them.

The Buzz Words

As we're listening to your customers, we need to listen for certain buzz words. This is the point in the call when we discover which buttons to push and when to push them in order to guide the customer into realizing that it was their idea to buy from us in the first place. When they talk about the product that they are currently using and they complain about the price, for example, we know immediately where to position our product with respect to price. We've already done our homework and know about all of our competition, so we know about their product before they even tell us. We may even know how the competition distributes their product and how they collect their fees—in that case, we can listen for how the customer feels about the previous buying experience. In our recon, we should find out everything we can from our indestructible relationship(s) about how the company buys what we're selling and if this has caused problems with our competitors. Are our competitors particularly good at the type of product delivery that we have?

The buzzwords that we're looking for are things that we need to know in order to best position our product. These buzz words will vary from customer to customer, and are rooted in our research and recon. If we ask the right questions, and listen to the customer, they will tell us exactly how to best position our product to win the sale. They will tell us what they think is a fair price, they will tell us that they trust us by their participation in the conversation, they will tell us how they prefer to pay and have the product delivered—all we need to do is listen, confirm that we understand, and explain how our product is going to significantly improve their business.

Chapter 6 Recap

- The customer must become a partner
- The partner always wins
- The partner must completely own the choice to buy

Magic for Thought

1. Have you ever played *Three Card Monte*? Has a salesperson ever convinced you of a sure thing?

2. If your customer chooses you, how will they win?

3. When was the last time you really listened to someone? What was that like

Chapter 7

Mastering the Basics
Animating the Plan
Guiding the Sales Call
Involving Your Partner
Casting Your Spell

Define the Close

A close for a call is not always—or perhaps even usually—the close of a sale. Not all sales managers will agree. But most of the time, if we're selling high-end products, we need to give the customer plenty of room to own their choice. So we need to set goals and know exactly where we need to be at the end of the call. It might sound crazy to the person who sells retail or a high pressure type smaller sales, but many larger type solution sales might take up to a year or two to close, and every call before closing advances the sale to the next step.

Sometimes the close might be defined for us. Some sales managers are high pressure, demanding high numbers from their salespeople and want their team to close, close, close. They live and die by the old ABC sales adage—always be closing. I've heard of managers who have wanted daily reports from their sales team, and every second had to be accounted for. This is undue pressure on higher-end sales teams. Pressure is ok for lower priced items like retail clothes and cars, but pressure is bad for higher priced items. This is a very important factor to remember.

Sales pressure is directly related to complexity of sale.
Simple sale = high pressure
Complex sale = low pressure

Fortunately, the smarter and more seasoned sales managers let their sales team work their magic without too much interference. I believe that salespeople are running their own business, and if we don't approach it as our own business, we won't succeed. In higher priced sales, we'll need to be self-motivated to make a lot of calls over a longer period of time, so smart sales managers will often leave the sales team alone on the condition that they meet their numbers. The decision makers need to take their time to make their choice because so much is on the line. Pressuring them will backfire, and pressure on the sales team will cause them to pressure the customer.

Whenever I have been in management positions or have had people working for me in my company, I have always let my people know that I preferred to be considered their partner, not their boss. For them to buy into the philosophies and goals of the company, they need to be a partner just like a customer does. A boss dictates what someone should do; however, a partner or mentor creates or instills the power of creativity and ownership. If a person is empowered with a sense of ownership a certain kind of magic occurs. The individual tends to want to grow and prosper for themselves and the company.

I coach Little League T-Ball and one player sticks out vividly for me. For about the month of the season I had monumental challenges with this one kid. He was a very good player but he would goof around, wrestling, talking, and not paying attention to what was happening. It began to affect the other kids and their performance in a negative way. I had tried everything I could to maintain control but was beginning to get really frustrated. Then I had an idea.

I pulled him aside after practice one day and told him he was one of the best players on the team and that I needed his help. I told him that I needed him to help the younger kids learn the game and how to play it as well as he does. For the first time in the entire season he looked directly in my eyes and listened to me—smiling. Form that day forward, I had a model ball player and a genuine leader for our team.

It's best to define the close long before the call. We need a pipeline of customers for the year—based upon typical averages, we should get about 80% of our business from about 20% of the pipeline. As magicians, we are looking to grow that percentage. Then, we'll prioritize the customers based on the percentage of business that they will bring us, and work our way through the list. As we're doing our research on our customers, we can get an idea for how many calls we'll need to make to close the sale, outlining the people that we'll need to win and the buying process that our particular customer has in place at the company. In the end, our research and recon will tell us who we need to talk to, and the sales cycle will determine when. We will be visiting with higher-end customers a lot. Indestructible relationships are not built in a day, and we're going to need them.

When it Goes Sideways

We might try every tactic in the book and still not be able to soften a customer—to convince him/her that we really want them to win on the deal and get the product that serves them best. There are some people that we just won't be able to break, and that's ok, we'll get better with practice. There are people that even the best salesperson in the world couldn't touch, and there's no salesperson with a perfect or even near perfect game, so every salesperson has lost. Most have lost a lot. And the best have lost even more.

Don Schlitz penned the now famous words—thanks to Kenny Rogers—about the life of a gambler:

You've got to know when to hold 'em
Know when to fold 'em
Know when to walk away
Know when to run

143

That guy I saw in New York—the one who lost all his money to a game of *Three Card Monte*—didn't know when to walk away, and he should have run. This cost him at least a couple hundred bucks, and God knows what else. Did he have the money to lose? What about his family? One of the signs that should have given it away: he was bleeding money. The dealer wasn't shy about the scam—he was in a high-pressure situation where he had to get as much money as he could as fast as he could because the unfortunate tourist wouldn't be coming back. But the dealer had just enough talk in him to make the game irresistible. The point here is simply this: walking away can save you from an unfortunate end.

Even when we feel the sale starting to slip away, we still might be in the game. I've told the story of a customer that melted when I joked about my birthday, which happened to be his as well. The difference is uncanny—instead of listening to me with an attitude of indifference and suspicion, he now listened with genuine interest because I made a simple personal connection. At this point in the pitch, we can ask frankly, 'What are your concerns about moving forward?' We're asking this question to confirm that the customer fully understands what we've said about the product. Then there's the fully loaded question, 'I want to make the decision process as painless as possible for you. What can I do to make that happen?' If they answer the second question, we've got the sale. We may need to make another visit or two in order to make good on our promise, but this is a very good thing because we're one giant leap closer to closing.

However, if we're getting unmistakable signals that they aren't going to buy from you—like when we find out that there's an important person in the group who is determined to sabotage our efforts (which is very rare) or if the customer *always* goes with someone else, or if we cannot win the interest of the customer, and especially if you're talking with the wrong person, it's time to move on with the firm optimism that tells you that you will do better next time.

When we get the 'no,' it's important to remember that it's not the end of the relationship. A lost sale today can be a valuable customer tomorrow. So we always keep the door open—and we ask to keep it open. No matter who they buy from, we can leverage our indestructible relationships (or in some cases, the best relationship that you have) and follow up to make sure that the product is good for them. We always keep in touch to see when they're buying again so we can have a seat at that table.

No matter what happens during a particular sales cycle, we can take away something valuable for our next customer. We often learn more from our loses than we do from our wins. Build an exit interview—a set of questions for your best contact to see what went wrong during the pitch. What is it that we could have done better? Did we blow it or were they never really considering us in the first place? What went wrong? What did we do that was perfect for our team (as we know, there's always something, right)? I let my customers tell me what I did wrong so I can get the sale next time.

Whether things go right or wrong for me, I always leave a positive footprint—my personal brand. I always close with the same lighthearted comment (as I mentioned earlier), and people remember me for it. It's a good conversation starter when I see them again, and after a while we can really become good friends. My little joke is a sort of trademark—I can time it perfectly and get the kind of reaction I'm looking for. This is a good thing to work out with a partner in role-play. Your footprint doesn't need to be funny, and I haven't done my job if they can't remember anything more from the presentation. However, it does help them to recall the content fondly. If they don't remember you for something positive, they won't be able to distinguish you from the other guy.

Not Closing the Sale

Most of our sales calls will not lead to a close. We've heard that 80% of our business will come from 20% of our clients. Now this standard slides with the value of the product. Someone who is selling retail needs a much higher percentage, and the folks who are selling super-high end products will see 80% of their business coming from 4% of their clients. By these numbers, we are going to hear the word 'no' a lot more than we will get the 'yes.'

Each of us deals with rejection differently. It's perfectly normal to feel bad about losing a sale. We are extensions of our products, so in a very real sense, they are not only rejecting the product, they are rejecting us. Thank God for our *Captain Solution* invincible force field. In addition to this, we have invested time and energy into the sale. We've done everything right, but the numbers are difficult to escape: 80% of your calls will not close. This can challenge our ability—among other things—to smile all the time and laugh with our customers. Of course, friendliness *can* be faked, but if it's discovered, we've lost the sale. It's good to have a light switch, believing that you have your 'A' game on when you're really off. A good actor can play Hannibal on the set, but come home and be himself. If you're an actor playing the part of a salesperson, you won't take failure personally because you'll go home and be yourself.

There is no meaningful success without failure. Babe Ruth hit a career total of 714 home runs out of 2,873 hits. That's a 24.5% success rate. And the Sultan of Swat sits pretty at the 105th all-time strikeouts in MLB history with 1,330. The Babe always swung for the home run—he famously said, "If I'd just tried for them dinky singles I could've batted around .600." His actual batting average was about half that, which is still very good, at .342. The mighty Reggie Jackson tops the all-time strikeout list with a dazzling 2,597. 2,598 if you include the Reggie Bar. The list boasts other legendary hitters such as Jimmie Foxx, Cal Ripken, Jr., and Willie Mays, all of whom had a much lower success rate than the Bambino. The greatest mistake in baseball history was when Harry Franzee of the Boston Red Sox sold the Babe to the New York Yankees, where he led the team to seven pennants and four World Series championships. In the mean time, the Red Sox suffered 86 years without a World Series win. Franzee's blunder has been called "The Curse of the Bambino," and only recently has the curse been lifted. The Boston Red Sox waited more than eight decades to win a World Series, and have amassed three World Series Championships in the last decade. Alas, we have persevered!

There is a secret to not letting loss get to you: if you take care of your personal life and you're genuinely happy without closing the sale. It's a matter of setting goals that enrich your life, pursuing these goals, and enjoying them.

What I do is this: I set goals that I can achieve within a certain timeframe, write it down or get a picture of it and tape it to the mirror in my bathroom. If your goals are things that enrich your life: a new car, a boat, something nice for the family, or a vacation, this is an indication that you are in the game for the right reasons. You have a positive motivation to close sales, and after you enjoy the fruit of your efforts with your family, it motivates you even more to be successful. When your goal is constantly centered on getting more money, you can be sucked in to all manner of unethical practices in the name of the dollar. Customers become numbers that you cannot relate to, and your pipeline will be poisoned by an inability to build indestructible relationships that makes your sales career durable.

This is the difference between the "good guy/girl" and the "bad girl/guy" that we talked about earlier. The "bad guy/girl" gets beat down by sales that don't close, and gets hungrier and more desperate as time goes by—a "good girl/guy" can continue to build under such conditions, reaping a harvest out of unlikely situations. You will be able to tell the difference within yourself: can you look in the mirror and see a person who is physically and spiritually healthy? Or do you see a person who is selfish, burnt-out, or even dishonest? It may well be that only you know what you're doing is wrong—it might not be illegal *per se*, but it could be unethical, and this is a weak foundation for sales.

Ethics

Everything that we needed to know about sales ethics we learned in kindergarten. And that's true. Sales ethics is not complicated. This doesn't mean that you'll find yourself in odd situations where a choice is not black and white. However, there are two guiding principles that should govern our choices.

- Ask yourself if your course of action serves the customer.
- If you were the customer, would you want a salesperson to do what you're doing?

If we put the needs of the customer before our own, and the customer knows this, we have a significant advantage in every stage of the sales cycle. They will no longer be suspicious of us because we have shown them that we want them to win during every call. We're not just putting their needs first when we face an odd choice—we have to build up this trust from the beginning. Because of this, we'll be able to talk about their needs rather than price, get answers to our leading questions, and show them just how serious their needs really are.

There's the second guiding principle, which is in so many philosophies and world religions that it's called the **Golden Rule**: *If you were the customer, would you want a salesperson to do what you're doing?* We've already done some of this in our preparation for the call: we've role-played the customer/salesperson with our colleagues or gracious family members. It's very important to role-play, because we'll find out what works and what doesn't work before we go into a call. So the rule is somewhat at work, because we've already explored the customer's wants and needs. When we're making choices, simply consider the other person's wants and needs, and you'll be on the right track to closing a mutually beneficial deal.

In magic, I can give two examples of unethical behavior. I'm sure that you've heard that a magician never reveals the secrets of magic—except to another magician. Because of this credo, it's very difficult to find books and learn new tricks or effects. There's a level of skepticism and distrust of the curious because the secrets are so precious. So the first example of unethical behavior in magic, and the only grounds for excommunication from the world of magic is to cheapen these secrets. The most famous current example is someone you may remember from recent television shows, the Masked Magician, who has made a name for himself by exposing magic tricks. For other magicians, this is like walking into a dog park and kicking puppies. And he's banking on the fact that magicians don't want him betraying their secrets: it sucks the life right out of the essence of magical entertainment.

The second unethical practice is lying about the nature of magic. That is, the art of mentalism – telepathy and such – are not supernatural or paranormal. It's just like riding a bike: anybody can do it provided they are willing to learn, which includes falling down a few times. Do I believe that there are certain abilities that remain untapped for many of us? Absolutely. But I also believe that it's unethical for individuals who study the art of magic to take advantage of people and say that they can communicate with the dead or cure illness with a wave of the hand, etc. This is not misdirection for entertainment, it's stealing people's money if you're claiming to do something that you can't do. When I see or hear of magicians doing this, I have to shake my head and hope that they aren't going down a path that they'll regret. I know that I couldn't look myself in the mirror having convinced someone that I've talked to their dead husband or wife, when in fact it was just a 'sleight of hand' or a well-refined ability to read or influence people and their personalities.

Closing

Some salespeople are afraid to close the sale because they don't want to pressure the customer. Closing the sale is like telling the punch line to a good joke. Just as with a sale, there's a lot that can go wrong with a joke. If we wait too long to deliver the punch line, the listener loses interest. If we laugh too much too soon, the listener gets distracted. If we tell the wrong punchline to the joke, the listener cannot understand why we think it's funny. We can't even get to the punchline if you tell the joke out of order. But if we tell the joke just right and deliver the punchline at the right time, that's when the real magic happens.

So this example begs the question: how do we tell good jokes? Practice. Good magic effects require a lot of interaction with the audience. The novice magician's biggest mistake is rushing through everything. The story is told too fast and the audience cannot participate and own the show. The effect is choppy and clumsy rather than sleek and flawless. Worst of all, the novice magician fails to entertain when he/she does not time everything correctly. The seasoned magician knows that the audience must be engaged with the trick or misdirection will not work—the audience needs to think that they are participating by choice.

Like a joke, every magic effect is a narrative. The *cups and balls* effect is an ancient story that a magician tells, and has to capture the imagination of the audience and retain it long enough to deliver the effect, and each effect contributes to the show, leading to the finale.

Chapter 7 Recap

- Define the close
- Be the "good guy"
- Close when the customer is a partner who knows that they will win

Magic for Thought

1. What are the different levels of close for your sales cycle? (What is the 'next step' as you define your close?)

2. How do you keep from going over to the dark side, misdirecting customers as a way of life?

3. What are three ways that you've lost a sale, and what can you do to improve.

Chapter 8

Being a Sales Magician

If you follow the MAGIC method, you will be a sales magician. Everyone starts out at the same place with magic—a novice. Only with practice and careful application of method will a novice become a master—the apprentice will become the wizard when s/he can finally perform magic with the expertise of his/her teacher. Earlier in the book I mentioned the difference between a Golden Retriever and Ug, the ugliest dog in the world. Golden Retrievers are so cute and well-behaved that they can jump to the head of any line and win just about every heart. Ug has to work hard at dispelling all of the prejudices about ugly dogs and eventually people will see him as a yellow Labrador Retriever, which is not quite a Golden, but just as effective in winning friends. Some people are born salespersons and don't need to be as diligent in practicing sales techniques. The rest of us need to pay careful attention to every component of the sale—the research, development of the pitch, building indestructible relationships, guiding the customer through the sale, and closing the deal. The secrets of the MAGIC method focus on every aspect of the sale, setting both the novice and the expert salesperson on the path to strengthening their relationships and increasing their sales.

For those of you who just flipped to the back of the book to read this last chapter—I'm a mind reader—did you think I wouldn't know? Go back and read the book, it's worth it.

The Pillars of the MAGIC Method

The MAGIC method is built on three pillars: reading, study, and preparation. These pillars have made appearances in most of the MAGIC method, and in practice, these pillars weave the method together and give it life. Every professional reads, and most professionals read *a lot*. While Golden retrievers make it look easy—and truly, it is easy for them—the sales cycle can be frustratingly complex because the entire process is rooted in human relationships. Sales is just as maddeningly complex as the human being, including personality, psychology, physiology, neurology, and everything else that affects the function of human connection and decision making. There are many, many great books available on these and related topics. That's not to mention all of the wonderful works that directly address sales, business, and positive motivation. You could fortify yourself in the corner of a library and never come out, but you're going to have to if you're going to improve your sales.

The second pillar of the MAGIC method is study. This is a bit simpler than reading because you're not singlehandedly trying to unravel the human soul. In the discipline of study, you have already identified books that benefit you the most, and you re-read them attentively, memorizing the key points, working their lessons into the fabric of your sales practices.

The third pillar of the MAGIC method is preparation. In the MAGIC method, preparation is active, not passive. Preparation does not mean sitting at your computer mapping out your pitch, building on the notes from your research. The level of preparation that you need in order to practice the MAGIC method includes developing an elevator pitch, role-playing, and carefully outlining every element of the sales call. Magicians read deeply, study diligently, and prepare exhaustively. The purpose for all of this preparation is to help the magician to effectively control his/her performance in spite of all the craziness that will happen in a live show. The salesperson that is well prepared will be able to retain at least the appearance of control no matter what happens during a sales call. Good preparation allows the salesperson to focus on other things—like the customer's needs, for example—rather than consciously trying to maintain control of the call.

Personalities

Identifying the personality types, and appropriately interacting with them, is an important part of practicing the MAGIC method. I used part of my egg effect to show you how I identify personality types. It might seem intimidating at first—there are many types of eggs just as there are many types of people. However, once you get the hang of it—with practice, you'll be an egg chef.

Mastering the Basics

The most important "basic" is listening. Like everything else in the MAGIC method, we're talking about *active* listening. There's a fundamental difference between listening and hearing. Hearing is an organic process. If you have functional ears, you can hear anything that's close enough and in the right frequency. If you have a hearing problem, you get that fixed by seeing a doctor and maybe getting a hearing aid of some kind. Listening involves comprehension, understanding, communication, and interaction. Listening is a discipline. If you have a listening problem, the only remedy is to learn how to listen and practicing it.

For the salesperson, listening means not talking. You may think you hear what your customer is saying when you're talking. But unless you have some superhuman power, you will talk yourself out of a sale if you talk too much, and too much is not much. That is, you can talk yourself out of a sale even if you feel like you're talking less than you should. In fact, you should talk less than that and listen more. I suggested that you develop an anchor, and use that anchor to keep yourself from talking. I use physical discomfort—I pinch the flesh between my thumb and forefinger to remind myself to listen. Whatever the customer has to say is more important than whatever you could say—they are telling you how to make the sale, so you'd better pay attention

Listening carefully empowers you to stay in control of the call. When the unexpected happens, you'll have everything they've previously said to you to help you guide the call. By listening to the customer, you'll learn their needs and attitudes, which will help you position your product. While it's basic, listening just might be the most important thing that you do during a sales call. Without it, everything else is meaningless.

Animating the Plan

Every plan needs life. We've all seen salespeople who have tried to give a lifeless pitch. The MAGIC method is designed specifically to breathe life into your sales methods. The thrill of the sale will serve as inspiration and motivation—there's just something about successfully guiding a call and winning a partner. In magic, there's nothing more thrilling than captivating an audience from the beginning to the end of the show. When you know that you've made the impossible *appear*, and the audience only wants more, you know that you are a real magician.

Proper positioning gives life to a sales pitch. This is where your research comes into play. You need to know not only your product inside and out, but also that of all your competitors. There is only one variable in positioning your product: the opinions of your customer. As you are listening to your customer, you will need to root out what the customer thinks of their current product—which may or may not be yours—and what they think can remedy the problem. Champion a solution for them. Your customer needs to know all of the wonderful things that your product can do for them, but if your product is not positioned well in their perception of the market, you're essentially speaking a different language. Your product needs to fit within a niche that your customer understands, and in order to do that, you need to listen carefully to what the customer has to say.

Guiding the Call

This is where I have the most fun. In order to master this part of the call, we need to be invisible—be in control without appearing to be in control. The magician is a master of guiding the call—getting the audience to buy in to the trick without even realizing it. The comic magician uses a kind of self-deprecation to guide the call, appearing to mess up on purpose, but the audience is unknowingly driven to an unexpected and (hopefully) wonderful conclusion, and all of the supposed goofs are carefully planned.

A key component to closing a sale is leading the customer to own the decision to buy from you. The customer needs to be confident that they decided that your product best solves their problems. In guiding the call, the salesperson asks guiding questions to lead the customer to the point of realizing that you're selling what they need. Your research will inform this process, and it's very likely that you'll know the shortcomings of their current product, and how your competitor's products can't meet their needs as well as yours.

Involving your Partner

Before you close the sale, your customer will become a partner. Involving the audience is one of the joys of being a magician. It allows me to win over the audience in the best way imaginable: by including them. This is a tried and true method that almost every magician uses, because by partnering with the right person in the audience, the magician has an advocate to help him/her win over the crowd. The partner can develop into an indestructible relationship, which for magicians means that we can rely on them for the rest of the show. They will be verifying that indeed the chains and locks are real, there's no escape from a box, and holding props, helping me carry along the audience until the finale. That's why we build relationships—the sale depends on human connection, and relationships are established connections. It is during this part of the sale that the customer realizes that they are going to win if they partner with you.

Casting Your Spell

And finally, the close. Some sales managers and many salespeople live for the close. However, on larger sales, most of the sales calls shouldn't end with a close, but they set the stage for the next step to the close, moving the call forward. Information needs to be gathered, relationships need to be built and nurtured, and more than one committee meeting might be need to set their minds at ease, making them perfectly comfortable with you and your product. With larger sales, more is at stake for the customer. Their reputation might be on the line—or maybe even the future of their company. So these customers need to have all of their questions answered without pressure from their salesperson.

Every aspect of the MAGIC method prepares you for closing:

- You've *mastered the basics* so you know everything that you need to know to position your product effectively and you know personality types so you can interact with people effectively

- You've *animated the plan*, breathing life into your pitch by listening effectively

- You've *guided the call*, asking leading questions to guide the decision making process while encouraging the customer to own the choice to buy

166

- You've *included your partner,* letting them know that you want them to win, and they will win if they buy from you

- You're ready to *cast your spell,* closing the deal at the right time

Many salespersons are afraid to close because they don't want to pressure the customer. While you certainly don't want to close at the wrong time, walking away from sales is no way to live. Your spell must be cast at the right time, and there are certain things to watch for—there are ways to know that the pressure is relieved and you can start processing the close.

- There are no doubts about you—your partner trusts you

- There are no doubts about your product—your partner has said that your product will meet their needs and improve their business

- There is no doubt about the win—your partner is confident that they are winning

Making Magic - The Next Step

Reading this book and applying its techniques to your sales strategy is the first step of a long, prosperous journey. We've seen that no magician is born—they are made through careful practice. Dedication to the craft guides the magician from nothing to a master of the magical arts. The evolution of a magician is similar to the evolution of a professional salesperson.

The professional magician is typically on a quest to develop tricks into effects, but it doesn't stop there. As I mentioned in the beginning of the book, s/he also is usually on a quest to find true magic. This quest naturally uncovers things that are not always evident to either the magician or the general public. The magician becomes a student of the science of human psychology, things that pertain to how we humans perceive and react to our environments. Points of interest include how we interact and communicate with one another, how we learn and remember, and how we connect with the world around us.

As all of these things are unearthed the magician's desire to learn more about these things delves into hypnosis, body language, facial expressions, and linguistic study. Oddly, there comes a point where magic begins to morph and blend into things not yet fully explained or understood... real magic reveals itself.

Paralleling this, the professional salesperson realizes a transitional path from a products-based sales concept towards a much more intricate, solution-based sales comprehension. The sales method we use will become increasingly deeper. Because of this, the connection with the customer becomes significantly stronger. You begin to cultivate the indestructible relationship you're after because you have connected.

Finishing this book and applying the MAGIC method is just the first step on the path to exponentially increasing your sales. It takes more than just reading, but also generous study and practice to get the most out of the principles of MAGIC. I'm sure that you've noticed that building relationships should be your highest priority. As such, success with the MAGIC method begins and ends with your dedication to enriching yourself and your relationships with your customers and partners. So remember—take care of yourself. Be content, smile, and work with passion.

I have created a workbook that is attached to the end of this book as an appendix. Don't worry; you don't need to be a

Rhodes Scholar to complete it. The workbook is a tool to help you study the MAGIC method and get the most out of your reading experience. Why didn't we directly address this material sooner? Because study means going back to the material and reviewing it until it is most useful to you. I want this book to be useful to you not only on the first read, but the second, third, and fourth read. The principles of MAGIC have shaped my life because I revisit them often, and they have been the key to my success in sales.

Even as this book is going to press, I am closing the biggest deal in my medical device sales career. It was a long, long sales cycle that afforded me time to develop several indestructible relationships with my partners. I was talking with one of my partners this morning and she told me something that resonates with the message of this book. She said something like:

> *You know, Chris, it's not about the product. There are several other companies that can provide basically the same product as your company at about the same cost. The reason why we chose your product is the relationship that several of us have developed with you.*

That is the message of this book in a nutshell. The MAGIC method is a step-by-step process that enables you to develop the kind of connection with customers that can produce indestructible relationships. Once that connection is made, people will want to partner with you, and you'll be on your way to your next big sale.

Harness the magic.

Appendix: The MAGIC Method Workbook

You are Becoming a Sales Magician!

The following pages comprise a workbook that guides you through the MAGIC method. If you complete the workbook, you'll be studying, and you'll see how wonderful the learning experience is. The pillars of the MAGIC method are reading, study, and preparation. You've read the book, now it's time to study a bit and work on your preparation. Then you'll be well on your way to exponentially increasing your sales.

Mastering the Basics
Animating the Plan
Guiding the Sales Call
Involving your Partner
Casting Your Spell

The first secret of the MAGIC method is *Mastering the Basics*. There are a lot of basics. What do you feel is the most important?

_____

_____

In magic, there's a tremendous difference between a trick and an effect.

For a magician and a salesperson, the key to mastering the basics is _____.

A salesperson is an _____ acting like a salesperson.

The salesperson needs to truly believe and know that he/she's the "_____."

Misdirection is one of the key elements that a magician must master. Misdirection is the art of keeping the audience's attention where the magician wants it. There are great uses of misdirection on a sales call:

- *Keeping the customer focused on the good qualities of the product*

- *Asking leading questions to get the customer to open up, even if you know the answers*

- *Eliminating physical barriers*

- *Ask leading questions about what they are currently using so they feed you information about disadvantages of competition that you already know.*

What happens when misdirection fails and the salesperson loses control of the call?

_____

_____

_____

The MAGIC method is a combination of tried and true sales methods and the secrets of magic. When you think of a magician, what images come to mind?

_____

_____

_____

In magic, there's a tremendous difference between a trick and an effect.

Magicians aren't _____ they are

_____.

Magic can make Ug the ugliest dog in the world into

_____.

A few salespeople are born, but with

_____ anyone can make sales magic.

The MAGIC method is built on three pillars: read, prepare, study. Most professionals read quite a bit. Think about the last few books that you read...

What are the last three books that you read, and have you returned to them for study?

_____

_____

_____

Think about the most influential book that you've ever read -- what has this book done for your business?

_____

_____

_____

About Price...

Has there ever been a time where you've lost a sale because you revealed the price at the wrong time? Have you ever not closed with someone who made this mistake? Why was price discussed at the wrong time?

_____

_____

_____

To price or not to price....

We don't want to reveal our price until we've made our

product _____ to our customers.

The _____ the price is, the _____ we can reveal it.

Learning gestures can put you far ahead of the curve in a sales call. You will see that your customers will clearly tell you how they are receiving your pitch and what you should do next.

In this exercise, match the gesture, its meaning, and your response. Only one of these items is given for each gesture - see how well you do by comparing your answers with the personality chart above. Please don't limit yourself to the chart in the book -- be yourself and put it in your words so you can use it effectively.

I suggest that you work on this with a pencil.

GESTURE	MEANING	RESPONSE
1. Touch nose		

Example: The missing gestures, meanings, and responses are given in italics.

GESTURE	MEANING	RESPONSE
1. Touch nose	*agreement or hurry up and finish*	*Ask a confirmation question (How does this sound to you)*

Gesture Exercise, part 1. Match the appropriate meaning, response, and gesture.

GESTURE	MEANING	RESPONSE
1. Touch middle finger		
2.	Fear	
3. Backing away		
4. Touching watch		
5.	Losing Interest	

Gesture Exercise, part 2

GESTURE	MEANING	RESPONSE
1. Touch nose		
2.		Ask a confirmation question
3.		Make sure you are not building pressure
4. Touch ring finger		
5.	Eomotional (positive)	

Listening is asking leading questions. You want to listen to your customer's needs far more than you talk, but you should still guide the conversation with your questions. I gave several examples of leading questions that I ask.

- I always begin by asking customer where they are and how did they get there.

- What did the company use before you got here?

- Is there any resistance to change from your staff? [or anyone else, depending on the situation]

- If you could change one or two things about your product, what would that be?

- What do you really like about your current product?

What leading questions can you ask your customer to guide the conversation?

_____

_____

Be Indestructible

Cultivating indestructible connections with our customers can produce tremendous benefits. Over the years, my indestructible relationships have produced:

- Letters of reference

- Feedback and ideas for new products

- Information about what the competition is doing

- Let me know what is working in my sales strategies

How are your indestructible relationships working for you now?

_____

_____

_____

A mile in their shoes

It's a very old saying and it's stayed popular because it's so wise. Unless you walk a mile in another person's shoes, you really don't understand them. We do this with out imagination most of the time -- how do you imagine your competition makes sales calls?

_____

_____

_____

If you were your competitor, how would you sell their product?

_____

_____

_____

Mastering the Basics
Animating the Plan
Guiding the Sales Call
Involving your Partner
Casting Your Spell

The second step of the MAGIC method is breathing life into your sale. You are taking what other has done—the secrets of magic and sales—and adding your own personality.

What are you doing in your sales calls that are uniquely yours?

_____

_____

_____

Animating your plan involves effective positioning, active preparation, and consulting v. sales.

If you can communicate to your customer that you put their

needs first, explaining how your product works to this end,

you're no longer a _____ but a

_____.

Getting into position

In order to sell your product, you need to know how to position yourself in the market. Most of this will come from your research, but much of it will come from listening to your customer.

Where do your customers usually position your product, and how close is that to where you want it to be?

_____

_____

_____

In magic, there's a tremendous difference between a trick and an effect.

Proper positioning gives _____ to your sales calls.

You are an _____ of your product, so you're positioning yourself as well.

People want to buy products that are

_____ represented.

Role-play your best pitch ever

Let your partner score your elevator pitch on presentation and clarity.

DID THE SALESPERSON MEET THE OBJECTIVES	AGREE RATE 2-20	DISAGREE RATE 1-10
1. Do you understand the product well enough to buy it?		
2. Did the presentation inspire trust? Did you feel that you could trust the salesperson"		
3. Was it an elevator pitch that covered the major points of the sale or was it incomplete?		
4. Did the positioning of rhe product make sense?		
5. Was the salesperson comfortable with him/herself with presenting the product so precisely?		
TOTALS: GRAND TOTAL:		

Role-play your best pitch ever

Score your partner's elevator pitch on presentation and clarity.

DID THE SALESPERSON MEET THE OBJECTIVES	AGREE RATE 2-20	DISAGREE RATE 1-10
1. Do you understand the product well enough to buy it?		
2. Did the presentation inspire trust? Did you feel that you could trust the salesperson"		
3. Was it an elevator pitch that covered the major points of the sale or was it incomplete?		
4. Did the positioning of rhe product make sense?		
5. Was the salesperson comfortable with him/herself with presenting the product so precisely?		
TOTALS: GRAND TOTAL:		

Elevator Pitch Results

So you've done your elevator pitch. What does it all mean?

Score

-20	Shoot the messenger
-10	Eat your wheaties next time
0	Needs some work
10	Get a second opinion
20	Get revenge when it's your partner's turn
30	Ug the ugliest dog did a little better - we've all been here
40	You're a golden retriever
50	Your mother's opinion doesn't count

Mastering the Basics
Animating the Plan
Guiding the Sales Call
Involving your Partner
Casting Your Spell

Now the call is in our hands. We've done your research; we've practiced and role-played to refine our pitch. Now we're getting into the meat of the call.

Can you think of a time when a salesperson successfully guided you through a call? How did he or she do it?

_____

_____

Guiding the call takes one particular discipline...

_____ is the most important thing (and it's not asking questions).

When you get the urge to _____, ***don't!***

Solving their problems

What are some product-specific questions that you can ask your customers so they recognize their needs and want to buy from you?

_____

_____

_____

Mastering the Basics
Animating the Plan
Guiding the Sales Call
Involving your Partner
Casting Your Spell

You've heard that listening is asking leading questions. And we're still adding questions, this time focusing on how the customer wins by purchasing our product.

- How do those one or two things that you would like to change, if you could, affect your overall productivity on a daily, monthly, yearly basis?
- How does this affect your staff?
- Do you think it affects the morale, productivity and/or their job satisfaction level?
- If you were to all it all up, what do you think the overall cost factor to your organization's bottom line is?

How do you convince your customer that they are going to win when they buy from you?

_____

_____

Mastering the Basics
Animating the Plan
Guiding the Sales Call
Involving your Partner
Casting Your Spell

It's almost time to close. There are many types of closings for a sales call, and not every closing will end with a sale. Most sales calls simply advance the sale to the next level until you finally reach the end of the sales cycle and you make the sale.

- Define the close: how should this call end?
- Don't over close: keep talking after you've made the sale.
- Most sales will not close: know when to walk away
- Be relentlessly optimistic: laugh with them and smile with a passion

Are you happy with your sales numbers now? Why?

_____

_____

_____

Bibliography

Tony Alessandra, *Charisma*. Warner Books, 1997.

Philip Delves Broughton, *The Art of the Sale... Learning from the Masters About the Business of Life.* Penguin Books, 2013.

Dale Carnegie et al., *How to Win Friends and Influence People in the Digital Age.* Simon & Schuster, 2012.

Christopher Chabris and Daniel Simons, *The Invisible Gorilla* Crown, 2010.

Steve Cohen, *Win the Crowd.* Harper Resource, 2005.

Milo O. Frank, *How to Get Your Point Across in 30 Seconds or Less.* Simon & Schuster, 1986.

Timothy J. Koegel, *The Exceptional Presenter.* Greenleaf Book Group Press, 2007.

Jeff Koser and Chad Koser, *Selling to Zebras.* Greenleaf Book Press, 2008.

Stephen L. Macknik and Susana Martinez-Conde, *Sleight of Mind*, Henry Hold, 2010.

Og Mandino, *The Greatest Salesman in the World.* Bantam, 1983.

Maria Montessori, *The Absorbent Mind*. Holt Paperbacks, 1985.

Peter Montoyo and Tim Vandehey, *The Brand Called You*. Personal Branding Press, 2003.

Niel Rackham, *Spin Selling*. McGraw-Hill, 1988.

Ronald M. Shapiro and Mark A. Jankowski, *The Power of Nice*. John Wiley and Sons, 2001.

Brian Tracey, *The Psychology of Selling*. Thomas Nelson, 2006.

Ron Willingham, I*ntegrity Selling in the 21st Century*. Currency Doubleday, 2003.

Jerry Weissman, *The Power Presenter*. Wiley, 2009.

Zig Ziglar, *Secrets of Closing the Sale*. Revell, 2004.

About the Author

Christopher Lee Tabora has entertained at world-class casinos, professional sports teams, and countless corporations. He has paralleled his magic career with more than twenty years of sales and sales management ranging from retail to Integrated Delivery Network and multiple hospital sales.

Chris met his wife, Michele, while they were working in the medical sales field and they have been partnering in their sales efforts and magic performances ever since. Chris and Michele's expertise in medical device sales are well received and highly sought after at the many sales seminars they present.

Chris also believes there really is true magic… it is the gift we all have but may not use to its full potential—the gift of making others smile.

30510860R00125

Made in the USA
Charleston, SC
17 June 2014